20 (*Surprisingly Simple*)
RULES *and* TOOLS *for a* GREAT DAY

Tyndale House Publishers, Inc., Carol Stream, Illinois

20 Surprisingly Simple RULES and TOOLS for a GREAT DAY

Library of Congress Cataloging-in-Publication Data

Stephens, Steve.
  20 (surprisingly simple) rules and tools for a great day / Steve Stephens.
    p. cm.
  ISBN-13: 978-1-4143-0584-4 (sc)
  ISBN-10: 1-4143-0584-2 (sc)
    1. Happiness—Religious aspects—Christianity.   2. Success—Religious aspects—Christianity.   3. Christian life. I. Title.   II. Twenty (surprisingly simple) rules and tools for a great day.
  BV4647.J68S74 2006
  248.4—dc22   2006028667

Printed in United States of America

12 11 10 09 08 07 06
 7   6   5   4   3   2   1

CONTENTS

Getting Started 1

RULE ❶ .... Pay Attention 5

RULE ❷ .... Live Intentionally 15

RULE ❸ .... Know Yourself 23

RULE ❹ .... Keep Balanced 31

RULE ❺ .... Let Go 43

RULE ❻ .... Reach Out 51

RULE ❼ .... Celebrate 61

RULE ❽ .... Dig Deep 69

RULE ❾ .... Work Hard 79

RULE ❿ .... Rest 87

RULE ⓫ .... Cling to the Positives 97

RULE ⓬ .... Draw Close to God 107

RULE ⓭ .... Cultivate Community 117

RULE ⓮ .... Be Committed 127

RULE ⓯ .... Look for Lessons 137

RULE ⓰ .... Accept Mystery 147

RULE ⓱ .... Shine Brightly 155

RULE ⓲ .... Nurture Peace 165

RULE ⓳ .... Watch Your Words 175

RULE ⓴ .... Leave a Great Legacy 183

Truly Live Life 191

GETTING STARTED

TODAY IS A GREAT DAY.

In fact, lately, every day is a great day.

A great life is built one day at a time; some days are smooth and some days are rough, but each day is significant. You never know what your day might hold:

- sickness or health

- tragedy or victory

- attacks or appreciation

- confusion or clarity

- catastrophe or predictability

- exhaustion or energy

It doesn't matter what your day holds, but it does matter how you approach each day. Included in this small book are twenty surprisingly simple ways to approach every day of the rest of your life.

Each day is a gift, an amazing gift. You can make it great—or you can passively let it go by. This book is about embracing the magic of each day, welcoming it as it fills you and empowers you and transforms you into something greater than you ever thought possible. To make your day great, you have to learn a few basic rules.

Life is full of rules. Some may be silly or insignificant or random, but others are important:

> Stop!
>
> One Way!
>
> Do Not Enter!
>
> Beware of Dog!
>
> Poison: Do Not Drink!

You would be wise to follow these rules. Break them, and you risk a negative consequence. Good rules aren't meant to frustrate or control you; they are there to help you be more successful.

If you follow them, you'll be amazed at how the twenty surprisingly simple rules presented in this book can make an ordinary day extraordinary and save a difficult day from complete disaster. I have discovered these practical, thought-provoking rules in my work as a psychologist over the past twenty-five years. In this role, I have often made it my goal to help people improve their lives one day at a time by changing their attitudes, stretching their perspectives, and focusing their energy.

This personal and professional experience is important, but it is not the most crucial thing. Everything I learn through experience, observation, and research I run through the grid of the Holy Bible. God's Word is my foundation; with it as my frame of reference, I know I will not stray far from the truth. And the truth is what ultimately matters!

Each chapter in this book explains one of the rules and shows why it's important. After each rule, you'll find three tools. I've included these tools because while information might make interesting reading, it's the application of that information that lifts your days above the typical levels of monotony and mediocrity. These three tools will help you to apply the rules:

> **Prayer:** a way to seek God's help in getting you on track and keeping you there
>
> **Passage:** a quotation from the Holy Bible to give God's perspective
>
> **Practice:** a few assignments to help you insert the rules into the ups and downs of everyday life

With the help of these tools, the twenty rules can change your day. Each rule is surprisingly simple, yet profound. Former president Ronald Reagan once said, "For many years now, you and I have been shushed like children and told there are no simple answers to complex problems which are beyond our comprehension. Well, the truth is, there are simple answers. There just are not easy ones." These twenty rules are not easy, but they are well worth our effort. Even though I have written this book, it doesn't mean I have conquered all the rules. In fact, I have broken every one of them many times. Yet I have found that as I learn to understand them, apply them, and build them into lifelong habits, I have grown.

By now you're probably ready to try a rule or two. As you apply each rule, you will be amazed to see your days

grow deeper;

grow better;

grow positive;

grow inspiring;

grow more and more meaningful.

RULE **1**
PAY ATTENTION

IT HAD BEEN an overwhelming week.

I was going to school, doing two internships, working two jobs, volunteering at church, repairing a house built in 1902, and trying to finish a complicated doctoral dissertation. I was twenty-six years old and attempting to do much more than was realistic or even rational.

On my way home from church one beautiful spring afternoon, I looked up and noticed I was driving through a red light. Before I could even finish the thought, a car broadsided me. Glass shattered and metal crumpled. I shook my body to make sure everything was working properly. Then I went to the other car and was relieved to find out that no one was hurt.

When the police officer arrived and checked out the accident, he pulled me aside and gave me a piece of sage advice: "When you're driving, you've got to *pay attention.*"

I can't tell you how many times parents and teachers had told me that. I heard it in anger, frustration, impatience, and sometimes even in jest. I was surprised to find that Solomon, the wisest man in the world, also used these words. "Pay attention and learn good judgment. . . . My child, pay attention to what I say. Listen carefully to my words" (Proverbs 4:1, 20).

In my role as a psychologist, it is my job to pay attention. As soon as someone walks into my office, I focus on his or her words, tone of voice, emotions, needs, concerns, beliefs, perspectives, history, relationships, openness, and body language. This requires focus, and it can be exhausting. Paying attention is not always easy; in fact, sometimes it is hard work. Yet the payoff is that we become aware of an amazing world of causes and consequences just below the surface. Life is incredible. It is rich and inspiring beyond our wildest imaginations, but we have to pay attention.

I am convinced that few of us have any idea what is really happening all around us. We don't look and listen with intentionality. We don't take time to slow down, and when we do, we still don't consider very carefully what is right in front of us. Maybe we are too distracted or lazy or worn out. Maybe we are looking at the wrong things or in the wrong direction. José Ortega y Gasset said, "Tell me to what you pay attention and I will tell you who you are." Sometimes we just don't know how to pay attention. Yet whatever our reasons, this is something we can change with a bit of effort. Here are three big areas in which we all need to pay more attention each day.

OPPORTUNITIES

Each day is filled with incredible opportunities, but most people don't pay enough attention even to see them. Every day, many doors of opportunity stand before us—and sometimes they are frightening, inconvenient, or out of our comfort zones. Several years ago I was approached to do a daily call-in radio talk show. My schedule was full, and I had no experience with radio. I had been a successful psychologist for twenty years and had spoken to hundreds of groups, but quite frankly, the idea of a talk show made me nervous. What if I was on the air and didn't know what to say? What if I made a mistake and a hundred thousand people heard it? What if I sounded foolish or uninformed? The what-ifs overwhelmed me until I asked myself, *What if God just opened a door of opportunity? Are you willing to trust him and walk through it, or are you going to slam it in his face?* I'm glad to say I walked through it and had an absolutely fantastic time for four and a half years, until God shut that door and opened another.

We are surrounded by opportunities beyond our greatest dreams. All we need to do is pay attention and seize the opportunities before us. Opportunities come in at least four varieties:

① **Easy opportunities:** things we feel competent at and capable of
② **Challenging opportunities:** things that stretch us and are out of our comfort zones
③ **Overwhelming opportunities:** things we can't do without the expertise or assistance of others
④ **Supernatural opportunities:** things that seem impossible (things we know we can't do without God)

We need to have all four of these types of opportunities in our lives. Unfortunately, many of us keep gravitating to the easy opportunities, rarely slipping into the challenging or overwhelming areas. Because of this, our days are ordinary and our lives are stunted. Grace Speare encourages us to "welcome every problem as an opportunity. Each moment is the great challenge, the best thing that ever happened to you. The more difficult the problem, the greater the challenge in working it out."

7

Every moment is a great opportunity with the possibility of being the best thing that ever happened to you. If we are willing to look to God, we will find him waiting to take us to unforgettable places of excitement and fulfillment and opportunities. So, as the captain of the guard told the prophet Jeremiah when he released him from captivity, "The whole land is before you—go wherever you like" (Jeremiah 40:4).

BEAUTY AND WONDER

Yesterday I went on a hike with my two sons, Dylan and Dusty, up the small creek behind our house. It was a sunny February day with a frosty nip to the air, but we were determined to go exploring. We battled through brambles, climbed over mossy rocks, and waded across chilly waters. We laughed and joked and had a great time. About a mile upstream, all three of us suddenly grew silent. We had just entered a secluded place where the creek cascaded and the mist lingered in the air. A small grove of stately cedars guarded the multiple shades of green ferns and ivies. As the sunlight filtered through the trees at the perfect angle that illuminated the water, we knew this spot was sacred. It was beautiful, incredibly beautiful.

Nature is amazing. We are daily surrounded by its awe, wonder, majesty, splendor, power, and terror, but so often we fail to pay attention. Jesus tells us to "look at the lilies" (Luke 12:27). It's like he's telling us to stop and think about the simplest aspects of nature—the details, the fine points, the nonessentials.

A friend once asked me the purpose of all the unique, beautiful flowers that bloom in unknown meadows and are never seen by humans. My mind flashed to a hillside I stumbled upon off a narrow gravel road at the

Arctic Circle in northern Iceland. It was ablaze with thousands of brilliant yellow and blue wildflowers. I wonder whether God creates all this beauty for his own enjoyment as well as ours. Annie Dillard wrote, "Beauty and grace are performed whether or not we will sense them. The least we can do is try to be there . . . so that creation need not play to an empty house." I want to be there, and I want to pay attention.

We have lost our sense of beauty and wonder. We have grown callous and complacent. We have become so preoccupied with ourselves that we miss the glory of nature. Paul Simon said, "These are the days of miracle and wonder." Yet we walk amid the beauty, unaware of its magnificence and message.

Henry Ward Beecher wrote that "beauty may be said to be God's trademark in creation." Yet we often pay no attention to his handiwork and then wonder why we can't feel his presence. We need to pray with Rabbi Abraham Joshua Heschel: "Dear Lord, grant me the grace of wonder. Surprise me, amaze me, awe me in every crevice of your universe. Each day enrapture me with your marvelous things without number. I do not ask to see the reason for it all; I ask only to share the wonder of it all."

GOD MOMENTS

The book of Genesis tells the story of Jacob's dream, in which he saw a stairway that was filled with angels and reached from earth to heaven. When he awoke, he declared, "Surely the LORD is in this place, and I wasn't even aware of it!" (Genesis 28:16). Jacob had a "God moment"—a point in time when he was keenly aware of God reaching out and touching his life. Most of us have had moments when we sensed that God had just done something amazing in our lives or when we sensed that God was present with us. Unfortunately, we frequently don't pay attention to these moments, so they come and go and are often forgotten. They should be remembered, treasured, and shared with others. They are an important part of our story and a significant reminder of God's grace.

Jim Caviezel will likely never forget one of his God moments. Jim played Jesus in the 2004 Mel Gibson movie, *The Passion of the Christ*. He dangled nearly naked on a cross in bone-chilling winds during the filming. He was struck by lightning during a re-creation of the Sermon on the Mount. A fourteen-inch gash was ripped into his back when the "soldiers" missed their mark during a scene of Jesus' scourging. He dislocated his shoulder while carrying the cross. Through all of this he became aware of God's presence and protection. Jim said that these experiences "forced me into the arms of God. That's the only place I could go."

In his book *The God Moment Principle*, Alan Wright discusses the following five kinds of God moments:

> **Amazing rescues:** moments when God protected us, healed us, rescued us, or made a way out for us
>
> **Holy attractions:** moments when God led us to a healthier path, enabled us to resist a temptation, or inspired us to take a higher road
>
> **Unearned blessings:** moments when God gave us an unexpected blessing or an undeserved gift

Revealed truths: moments when God spoke to us through something we heard, saw, read, or felt and conveyed truth about himself or our lives

Valuable adversities: moments when God sustained us through difficult times or made us stronger through tests of adversity

If we pay attention to all the God moments in our lives, we will be lifted above everyday, ordinary existence to a level of greater meaning, purpose, and perspective. Julian of Norwich, a fourteenth-century English writer, stated, "It is God's will for us to pay attention to all his past acts. . . . Only then shall we rejoice in God." God moments, whether big or small, give us a more accurate and meaningful perspective on life, while reminding us of his never-ending perspective.

Too often we miss the most important stuff of each day because we don't pay attention. In the book *God Is in the Small Stuff*, Bruce Bickel and Stan Jantz insist that "if you want to improve in any area of your life, you have to pay attention to the small stuff." Sometimes the tiniest details and seemingly insignificant pieces of your day can have an extremely significant impact. So throughout your day, from when you wake up to when you go to sleep, please pay attention.

TODAY'S TOOLS

Prayer

Dear God,

Forgive me for all the times I was too distracted, lazy, or self-absorbed to truly pay attention to you or your hand in my life.

Help me to face reality honestly with my eyes and my heart and my mind fully opened. Thank you for walking alongside me when reality is tough and for holding me close when reality is frightening.

Teach me patience as I wait for you to open the right doors, and give me the courage to walk through those doors you open. Thank you for all the opportunities you have set before me.

Amaze me with your wonders. Stimulate each of my five senses to the intricacies of nature in such a way that I am drawn close to you. Thank you for being the creator of so much beauty and for allowing me to enjoy it.

Wake me up to the times you directly touch my life. Help me to treasure these God moments, meditating on them for my own growth and sharing them with others for their encouragement. Thank you for each of these miraculous interventions and how they have had an impact on my life.

I praise you for caring enough to pay attention to someone as broken and insignificant as I am. Nudge me often so that I may develop the habit of always paying attention.

Amen.

Passage

We must pay more careful attention, therefore, to what we have heard, so that we do not drift away.
Hebrews 2:1 (NIV)

Practice

① What opportunities have you been faced with in the past month? Which did you pursue?

② Go to a place where you can enjoy nature. Relax and pay close attention to all the details and beauty of what surrounds you there.

③ Sit down with a friend and share three God moments you have experienced in your life.

RULE ❷
LIVE INTENTIONALLY

EVERY DAY IS FILLED with choices.

In 1845 Henry David Thoreau chose to move out of a comfortable home to live alone in the woods in a house he built himself a mile from his nearest neighbor. He lived there for two years and two months. When asked why he would do such a thing, he replied, "I went to the woods because I wished to live deliberately . . . and not, when I came to die, discover that I had not lived. . . . I wanted to live deep and suck out all the marrow of life."

Living each day intentionally makes all the difference.

Your life is the sum of all the choices you make. Madeleine L'Engle wrote, "It is the ability to choose which makes us human," and George Eliot adds, "The strongest principle of growth lies in human choice." Lack of choice leads to lack of direction, and that takes us nowhere. Not making choices or being passive gets us in a rut. The longer we stay in the rut, the more we grow stagnant. To stagnate is

- to lie dormant

- to be inactive

- to fail to progress

- to exist without motion

- to die slowly

Choices move us forward; they cause us to grow. Our choices demonstrate who we really are. They show our character and shape our destiny. Paul J. Meyer wrote, "Your choice is your power. . . . You never know how large the impact may be from a seemingly minor choice." One simple choice can send out ripples that change your life and the lives of those around you.

I hadn't seen Danny since we were both teenagers. He had been my next-door neighbor and grade-school buddy. He was smart, athletic, handsome, and a natural-born leader. When I ran into him again after many years apart, I gave him a big hug and said, "It's so good to see you. What have you been up to all these years?"

"You don't want to know," Danny told me as he looked at the ground. "I've spent a lot of time wandering from town to town, looking for work. I've picked apples, mowed lawns, pumped gas. But most of the time I've spent in jail."

"What happened?" I asked, shocked.

He looked me in the eyes with a tear running down his cheek.

"It's simple, really," he said. "When I was a kid, I had two close friends. You were my positive influence. Doug was my negative influence. When I was fourteen, I chose to spend my time hanging out with Doug. That was the dumbest choice I've ever made, and I have paid for it for the past thirty years."

I gave Danny another hug and said, "But today you can start making different choices." He smiled and said, "Thanks."

Choices are incredibly powerful, but they can also be frightening, because intentional, proactive choices involve risk. Yet it is only through risking that you can grow. Helen Keller put it simply: "Life is either a daring adventure or nothing."

Life is a journey, and each step is a choice. Some people refuse to start, or they panic along the way and stop. Others step forward randomly with their eyes shut. What I encourage you to do is to step intentionally with your eyes wide open. Solomon wrote, "Look straight ahead, and fix your eyes on what lies before you" (Proverbs 4:25). As Michael Molinos, a seventeenth-century Spanish martyr, wrote, "When a man sets out on a journey to a great city, every step he takes is voluntary; he does not need to say, 'I wish to go to the great city, I wish to go to the great city.' That first step is an indication of his intention. He journeys without saying it, but he cannot journey without intending it." Determine your destination, your direction, and the best way to get there. Then choose to start your journey. This is the beginning of a thousand exciting choices.

The setting for the movie *The Matrix* is a time in the future when most humans have shut their minds to what's really happening in the world. When the character Neo realizes this, he faces a choice that will change his life dramatically. He can take a blue pill, forget everything that has happened, and return to his comfortable, but false, life. Or he can take a red pill, wake up, and face a tough reality—but also have a chance to save all of humanity. Maybe our choices aren't as big as Neo's, but they are significant. We all must choose what to do with our time, energy, abilities, influence, and resources. These choices aren't always easy or obvious, but they are fundamental to everything else. So what color pill will you take?

CHOOSING TO FOLLOW GOD

Live intentionally rather than passively or haphazardly. Consider your options. Don't let the pressures or expectations of those around you force your hand. Colin Powell warned, "Be careful what you choose. You may get it." Think through the cost and consequences of your choices, but also recognize the cost and consequences of not choosing. There are times we all need help with our choices, regardless of our age or maturity. So find a friend, a counselor, or a pastor who can give you perspective and wisdom.

God wants us to live every day to its fullest. He wants us to make positive and proactive choices so we can fulfill our life purpose. Thomas Merton wrote, "We must make the choices that enable us to fulfill the deepest capacities of our real selves." God knows our capacities, and he wants us to let him use them. When he asks us to follow him, he wants us to stop what we're doing and step out. It might be uncomfortable and challenging and frightening, but God's way is ultimately the best and most satisfying way. He asked

- Noah to build an ark
- Abraham to leave his home
- Moses to free his people
- David to face Goliath

None of these were easy choices, but each of them led to something surprising. Noah was saved from a flood. Abraham became the ancestor of the Jews. Moses led the Israelites across the Red Sea to the Promised

Land. David defeated a giant and proved God's power. Without taking risks, none of these individuals would have accomplished what they did. Each of these choices by these ordinary people set in motion a series of events that made their lives extraordinary.

FREEDOM FROM FEAR

What keeps most people from living intentionally and making life-changing decisions is fear. Moses encouraged his people to "be strong and courageous! Do not be afraid. . . . For the LORD your God will personally go ahead of you. He will neither fail you nor abandon you" (Deuteronomy 31:6). Take a stand today and choose courage. Courage is not the absence of fear; it is taking positive action in spite of your fears. Archbishop Desmond Tutu said, "Being courageous . . . means acting as you know you must, even though you are undeniably afraid." If we're courageous, we'll seriously consider risk but not allow the risk to paralyze us. We might need to shift our path, but we won't need to run away or hide.

Courage moves us forward. It allows us to face life head-on and live life to the fullest. Ralph Waldo Emerson wrote, "Whatever you do, you need courage. Whatever course you decide upon, there is always someone to tell you that you are wrong. There are always difficulties arising that tempt you to believe your critics are right. To map out a course of action and follow it to an end requires some of the same courage that a soldier needs."

Not to choose courage is to cave in to cowardice or mediocrity. Our choices make all the difference. They can make us or destroy us; they can connect us with others or alienate us; they can build our character or tarnish it. They can lift us above our circumstances or sink us into the deepest despair. Some choices seem natural; others are made by sheer gut-wrenching willpower. But we do have choices. Living intentionally is broader than making choices to act a certain way or take a certain course. It involves making choices about our attitude.

ACCENTUATE THE POSITIVE

I've met all sorts of people in difficult situations, such as physical handicaps, painful marriages, broken hearts, financial ruin, and seemingly hopeless futures. And yet they hold a positive, uplifting attitude. I don't know how they do it. William James wrote, "The greatest discovery of my generation is that a human being can alter his life by altering his attitudes of mind." Abraham Lincoln said it more simply: "Most folks are about as happy as they make up their minds to be."

I asked one woman who had been abandoned by her husband how she kept such a positive attitude. She had three small children, no job, no home, no friends, no good options. She lived in her car and ate at a local homeless shelter. She smiled and said, "I'm not dead, my children love me, and things can't get any worse." You can always choose your attitude. John Maxwell wrote, "We choose what attitudes we have right now. And it's a continuing choice." In fact, your attitude is the most important decision you make each and every day. Your attitude might very well set the stage for every other choice you make.

As for me, I want to make strong, affirming choices. I want to live life to the fullest with courage and a great attitude. I don't want to waste my time or miss the mark or wake up someday only to wonder what I have been doing for the past ten years. I want to stretch and grow and love and in some way, no matter how small, leave this world a better place than when I entered it. I want to reach out and dig deep and shine bright. I want to know God and celebrate all there is to celebrate.

So join me on this journey, and start today. Wake up. Choose to live with purpose and direction. Choose to live intentionally and make choices daily to affirm who you are and what you believe. Ed Rowell said it this way in *Go the Distance*: "We will never get another chance at today. If we don't make intentional choices, based on our understanding of God's plan for our lives, we will be consumed by the purposes of other people. It's time to focus. We can't afford to wait until tomorrow. Set your course today and stick to it."

Yesterday I spoke to Jody, a twenty-three-year-old college student. She has a vibrancy and excitement about her that is contagious. Her dreams are clear, and her plans to achieve them are strategic.

"How do you start?" I asked.

With a soft smile and steely stare, she said, "You just have to go for it."

TODAY'S TOOLS

Prayer

Dear God,

Forgive me for all the days and opportunities I have wasted. Forgive me for allowing anxieties and distractions to keep me from what is best.

Teach me to be active and intentional and strategic with my choices.

Show me your purposes and direction for my life so that my choices become a true reflection of your will and your ways.

Grant me the courage to follow you wherever you lead and obey whatever you ask. Then give me the strength and determination to turn each of these choices into reality.

Thank you for trusting me with choices. Please come to my side with your wisdom and peace as I learn how, when, and where to make these choices.

Bless me as I daily choose attitudes, actions, and words that might glorify you.

Amen.

Passage

Today I have given you the choice between life and death, between blessings and curses. . . . Oh, that you would choose life.
Deuteronomy 30:19

Practice

① How does fear keep you from doing what you'd like to do?
② Write out three specific choices you would like to make during the next three months.
③ Find a person you trust who will meet with you weekly and keep you accountable in following through with your three choices.

RULE ❸
KNOW YOURSELF

YOU ARE UTTERLY AMAZING!

You are a miracle and a mystery!

You are "fearfully and wonderfully made" (Psalm 139:14, NASB).

As a psychologist, I have concluded that most people live their lives without ever knowing themselves at anything deeper than a fairly superficial level. Yet how can you truly connect with anyone else, or even God, unless you have at least some inkling of who you are? How can you make informed choices, grow as a person, or compassionately reach out to others unless you know what is inside your heart? Marcus Aurelius, a Roman emperor, said that a wise man gives himself "frequent self-examinations." Every day, I want to examine how I have spent my day, especially recognizing what I've done well and what I wish I could do over.

Maturity requires self-awareness, but this is not to be confused with self-absorption. To be self-aware is to acknowledge who we are before God. It is to look beyond outward appearance to the heart, thanking God for each of our assets and liabilities. As we do so, we can yield our abilities and talents to him, while he works through our wounds and weaknesses to make us more like him. Self-awareness allows us to see ourselves as God sees us. On the other hand, to be self-absorbed is to look upon ourselves as either more or less significant than reality dictates. Self-absorption stunts our growth, marginalizes those around us, and attempts to make God our servant.

Knowing ourselves does not come naturally or easily. We spend so much of our time distracted and overwhelmed by what happens *around* us that we don't take the time to consider what is *in* us. Who we really are deep under our skin is a bundle of beauty, terror, consistency, ambiguity, arrogance, and insecurity. We each embody the sublime contradiction of being created in the image of God but formed from the dust of the earth. As the image of God we are creative, intelligent, and spiritual, with the capacity for choice and moral excellence. Yet as the dust of the earth we have limitations and weaknesses, with the potential for woundedness, failure, and evil.

POTENTIAL FOR GOOD AND EVIL

We may not like to admit it, but we are a strange combination of good and evil, light and dark, hope and doom, health and sickness. Our attempt to understand ourselves begins with accepting, and even embracing, these opposites. It is only then that we can give ourselves fully to God and let him transform us into what glorifies him most. Yet to even look at some of these inner contradictions makes many of us uncomfortable. We want everything tucked into neat little boxes that explain all our feelings, words, and actions. Our personalities contain many patterns and tendencies, but there are also disturbing loose ends that don't fit into our little boxes like we think they should. The first step in knowing ourselves is accepting that each of us has weaknesses as well as strengths.

YOUR WEAKNESSES

We all dislike parts of ourselves. To be human is to be imperfect. Jean Vanier wrote, "Growth begins when we begin to accept our own weakness." To deny our weaknesses is to live a lie. These weaknesses show themselves in many ways. Some appear through our failures, frustrations, and fears. Others display themselves in our confusion and uncertainty. Still others haunt us through our woundedness. You cannot live without being wounded, whether sexually, physically, verbally, emotionally, socially, spiritually, or by your own choices.

However these wounds might have been inflicted, they are painful and leave scars that last a lifetime. We are all wounded. Some hide it better than others. Some lie about it, either to themselves or to those around them. Yet the truth remains that we are all weak and broken and wounded.

Every day we fall. It may be a slight stumble or a full face-on-the-floor flop. Our lives are replete with these all-too-real reminders of our humanity that leave us hoping for grace and dreaming of mercy.

Knowing ourselves involves owning our weaknesses, then being vulnerable enough to reveal them to others. In many ways the greatest gift we can give is our brokenness, our weaknesses, our woundedness. This gift allows us to reach out with understanding and compassion that we might not have had otherwise. Someone who has a history of sexual abuse might have a better understanding of young girls who have experienced the same sort of nightmare. A person who struggled with reading as a child often makes a great teacher because he or she knows just how hard some students must work to get through each class.

Without our limitations, we might very well lack the motivation, insight, and determination to help others overcome their own limitations.

It's our weaknesses that make us real and connect us with others. Yet most of all they force us to lean upon God, not only for his strength, but also as the source of all grace and mercy. God can redeem all our weaknesses and failures. And we learn the truth that Dallas Willard wrote about in *The Divine Conspiracy*: "Nothing irredeemable has happened to us or can happen to us on our way to our destiny in God's full world."

YOUR STRENGTHS

God has wrapped up something of value inside each one of us, yet most of us are more aware of our weaknesses than our strengths. Few will argue that we all have weaknesses, but our strengths seem harder to admit. An important part of knowing ourselves is facing the fact that "God has given us different gifts for doing certain things well" (Romans 12:6).

Everyone is gifted in at least one area. Some people have a way with words, while others have a way with numbers. Some have athletic abilities or musical talent or mechanical leanings. Some are natural leaders, while others are encouragers. Some see the big picture, and others love details. We are all different: creative people, social people, logical people, organizational people, and spiritual people. You might have one of these gifts or a number of them. Yet whatever type of person you are, you are blessed. If you're not sure where your abilities lie, these simple questions might help you identify your strengths:

- What areas are you naturally good at?

- What areas are fun and exciting to you?

- What areas do you get the most compliments in?

These are the areas in which you have been gifted. If you are still stuck, ask a friend or someone who knows you well to give you his or her opinion.

Once you've discovered and accepted your strengths, it is important to make sure you are using what God has granted you. Pope John XXIII said, "Concern yourself not with what you tried and failed in, but with what it is still possible for you to do." Take your ability and find a place to use it. If you are mathematical, get involved with numbers. If you are social, surround yourself with people. If you are organizational, start organizing. The saddest thing I see is when people spend most of their time doing things they struggle with rather than what they're good at.

To have a great day, spend as much time as you can doing what you're best at. In so doing, you will feel excited, energized, and fulfilled. Likewise, too much time spent in your areas of weakness will exhaust you, frustrate you, and suck the life out of you. Marilyn vos Savant, a woman with one of the highest recorded IQs in the world, wrote, "Success is achieved by developing our strengths, not by eliminating our weaknesses."

ONE OF A KIND

Like snowflakes and fingerprints, each of us is one of a kind.

In order to understand the gift of who you are, you must look inside the package. Aimé Césaire, a twentieth-century poet from Martinique, said that "the secret to staying young is to never stop searching for yourself." Yet to know yourself is not always easy. It is often your most difficult journey. Just when you think you know who you are, you surprise yourself by something you do or say. These surprises are sometimes splendid and sometimes shocking, yet they are a part of the marvelous mystery of who you are. Accept yourself, yet always be open to growth, allowing God to stretch you into all you can be.

On a shelf in my office sits a brass kaleidoscope with double wheels of different types of stained glass. Some of the glass pieces in these wheels are like beautiful, sparkling jewels, while others are quite ordinary. As I look through the eyepiece, I am amazed to see how these elements come together to create such an awe-inspiring collection of patterns. I love to sit back, spin these wheels, and get lost in the ever-changing images. One day my kaleidoscope slipped out of a little boy's fingers. My heart sank when I saw a large crack across one of the glass wheels, yet to my surprise this crack made the designs more intriguing and intricate than before.

My cracked kaleidoscope reminds me of the human condition. We are all made of beautiful strengths and ordinary traits, but it's the cracks of weakness that give us character. Instead of decreasing our value, the cracks make us all the more interesting. These cracks also force us to turn to God or turn back to God, for he is the only one who can meld them into wonder-filled patterns and keep them from shattering into useless shards of glass. So study your kaleidoscope, and look deep into its patterns. You might be surprised at all you can see. Each day I wish to see myself more clearly—my weaknesses and my strengths. And in so doing, I will know myself better so that I can live tomorrow more effectively.

TODAY'S TOOLS

Prayer

Dear God,

Teach me how to be more self-aware and less self-absorbed.

Lead me inward so that I may understand how you made me and how I may draw closer to you. Help me to see myself as you see me so that I will allow you to mold and shape me into whatever you wish me to be.

Show me my weaknesses so that I may lean more upon you. Also show me my strengths so I may be a better servant to you and those you bring into my world.

Forgive me for the times I have grumbled and complained about my weaknesses. And forgive me for those times my strengths have led me to pride or lack of love.

Even though it is hard to say, thank you for making me exactly who I am. Amen.

Passage

Have a sane estimate of your capabilities.
Romans 12:3 (Phillips)

Practice

① Write down three of your weaknesses. Then thank God for them and consider what positive elements these weaknesses might offer.

② Ask yourself the three questions on page 26. What do you think your strengths are?

③ Ask yourself who you are when:

> *you are all alone*
>
> *you are stressed*
>
> *everything is going your way*
>
> *nothing is going your way*
>
> *you are all God wants you to be*

RULE ❹
KEEP BALANCED

"I CAN'T DO IT!"

"Oh yes, you can," Aunt Sandy insisted.

My six-year-old hands gripped the handlebars of my bicycle, and my body tensed. "Please don't let go," I begged.

"You've got to learn to ride a bicycle sometime."

"But the road is too bumpy, and I'll crash."

"Hold on!" Aunt Sandy called as she ran alongside my bike. Then she gave it a strong push.

I went sailing down the road, holding on for dear life. I tried to reach the pedals so I could put on the brakes, but my legs were too short. The bike picked up a little speed as it went down a slight slope, and I panicked. I closed my eyes and prayed that I wouldn't die.

Crash!!!

I went directly into a tree. The bike fell over, and I scraped up my knee pretty badly. Through my tears I cried, "I did it. I kept my balance."

Aunt Sandy shook her head. "But you have to keep your eyes open."

When you first learn to ride a bike, keeping your balance is hard, but as you develop confidence and experience it gets easier. Now when I climb on a bike, I don't even think about keeping my balance. It just comes naturally.

Walking, jogging, skateboarding, climbing, reaching, and almost every simple movement you make requires balance. Every morning as you roll out of bed to stand up, sensors and receptors in your muscles send lightning-fast messages to your brain, which responds with the appropriate message to small stabilizer muscles in your feet. This process is called balance. Without it we would stumble, trip, flail, and definitely fall.

To a healthy, growing person, balance is much more important than physical coordination. Balance has to do with respecting each aspect of who we are. It means that we recognize the five key parts of ourselves:

① mind
② heart
③ relationships
④ body
⑤ spirit

Each of these parts is equally wonderful and individually holy. Each deserves time and focus. We are indeed the sum of our parts. After all, the word *health* comes from an old English word meaning "whole." As Pope John Paul II said, "Man always travels along precipices. . . . His truest obligation is to keep his balance."

Ever since I was a small child, I have been fascinated by starfish. I can remember searching the rocks and tide pools of Cannon Beach near my home in Oregon for these amazing creatures. One day I found a starfish that was missing an arm. It looked strange and lopsided; it had lost its symmetry and balance. It was still alive and held much of its beauty, but it just didn't look right. Fortunately, there was hope for the starfish that in time it might be able to regenerate its missing arm. We are each like a five-armed starfish. If our lost "arms" are not regenerated, it will be obvious that something important is missing.

Each of your five "arms" impacts every other arm. Your mind informs your heart, calming or inflaming your emotions. Your heart touches your relationships, pulling others toward you, pushing them away, or positioning you against them. Your relationships influence your body, relaxing or stressing it, draining or energizing it. Your body affects your spirit, lifting it up or weighing it down. The repercussions of this process can happen in reverse or in any other order, but the interdependence shows how important it is that you respect and care for each of these five arms.

TAKE CARE OF YOUR MIND

Your mind matters. In your mind you form beliefs that help you navigate through life. As you face the joys and hurts of existence, your beliefs are tested. These convictions become a road map and a dictionary for how to approach whatever you may face. As a road map they give you direction; as a dictionary they help you define and interpret your experiences. Over time you develop beliefs about every aspect of life, and these beliefs are reinforced through your attitudes, words, and actions.

If your mind becomes imbalanced or your thinking faulty, you are headed for trouble. Our decisions are often based on our beliefs. With irrational, immature, or untrue beliefs, we steer our lives onto the rocks. Thoughts such as *God is dead, Nothing really matters, People are all idiots,* or *I'm going to do whatever I feel like, whenever I feel like doing* it can lead to danger and depression.

To evaluate your thinking, you need to question and challenge each belief. This will help you correct your life course and redirect it into deep harbors, where the storms of reality don't do permanent damage.

Rational, mature, and true beliefs keep us on track in every aspect of our lives. They also lead to wisdom. For this reason, I daily attempt to nurture and reinforce right thinking. I hold strong to beliefs such as "God is good," "Prayer is powerful," "Loving others builds positive relationships," and "Hard work pays off." These beliefs may be simple, but they keep me strong and lead me to the best ports of call. As I take care of my mind, I also try to remember that even good thinking isolated from the other four aspects of personality can have unfavorable consequences. Healthy people must consider the impact their hearts, bodies, spirits, and relationships have on all they do. As we embrace right thinking, we develop wisdom. After all, the challenge for all of us is to use wisely what God has so graciously given us. So every day, use the following methods to keep your mind healthy:

① **Renew your mind** by correcting faulty thinking.
② **Stretch your mind** by considering all the amazing things around you.
③ **Focus your mind** by thinking about what is good and positive and right.

TAKE CARE OF YOUR HEART

In the book of Proverbs, Solomon talks a lot about the heart. He advised us to "guard your heart above all else, for it determines the course of your life" (Proverbs 4:23). Our hearts can become hard or broken, anxious or angry or jealous. Our hearts can also be cheerful or peaceful, compassionate or thankful or pure. Every day we experience a variety of emotions, which shows that we are alive and responding to life. As Helen Keller once said, "The best and most beautiful things in the world . . . must be felt with the heart."

Our hearts are precious, but at times they can hurt and trap and confuse us. Here are a few ground rules for dealing with emotions:

> **Listen to your emotions.** Don't be afraid of them; they are telling you something important about yourself. To deny or ignore your feelings is to isolate yourself from your own heart, those who wish to relate to you, and God himself.

> **Accept your emotions.** Don't reject your feelings or tell yourself that you shouldn't feel what you are feeling. Emotions can be messy and at times embarrassing or frustrating, but they are genuine.

> **Manage your emotions.** Be honest with your feelings; don't minimize or exaggerate them. Don't let them manage or control you. Let your mind and heart work together for a balance between the two.

TAKE CARE OF YOUR RELATIONSHIPS

We need people. Frequently they hurt us, make us angry, let us down, break our hearts, and drive us crazy, but we still need people. Loneliness is one of the most painful and disabling emotions we can feel. In the Garden of Eden, God said, "It is not good for the man to be alone"

(Genesis 2:18). Relationships keep us from being trapped inside of ourselves. They help us to stretch and grow and mature. They also protect us when difficulties come. Solomon reminded us that "if one person falls, the other can reach out and help. But someone who falls alone is in real trouble" (Ecclesiastes 4:10).

Healthy relationships nurture us. They give us connection and comfort. They allow us to communicate our hopes and dreams, along with our fears and anxieties. Relationships provide opportunities for us to offer care and to receive it. Although these are significant elements, the most important aspect of relationships is love. In his modern classic *The Purpose-Driven Life*, Rick Warren asserts that "life is all about love." He goes on to say that "life without love is really worthless." Jesus commands us to "love your neighbor as yourself" (Matthew 22:39). It's impossible to love apart from relationships.

TAKE CARE OF YOUR BODY

The body each of us was born with has certain characteristics and tendencies. We inherit specific genetic data that, in part, shapes who we are by designating things such as physical appearance, natural abilities, and personality traits. Some of these we like; some we don't really appreciate. We also have the ability to develop certain aspects of what we have inherited. We might strengthen our muscles, learn to play a musical instrument, or redeem negative aspects of our personality. Unfortunately, we must also deal with traumas, diseases, accidents, deprivations, and poor choices that impact our physical well-being. Some people have it easier than others. That might not be fair, but as my mother said many times, "Life is not fair."

We may not be able to control everything about our bodies or the factors that impact them. Yet there is much we can do. Taking care of ourselves is a statement of respect and thankfulness for what God has given us. Healthy bodies allow for healthy minds and hearts. They give us freedom to reach out to others and to God because we feel better, have more energy, and are less self-focused. Unhealthy bodies force us inward to care for our own diseases and disabilities.

TAKE CARE OF YOUR SPIRIT

Albert Schweitzer was concerned that many, if not most, people suffer from what he called the "sleeping sickness of the soul." In our physical, materialistic, rational, self-absorbed culture, have we lost our souls and spirits? Have we grown blind and numb to the spiritual universe that surrounds us? Are we like the servant at Dothan?

In one of my favorite stories of Scripture, this servant wakes up one morning to see enemy troops, horses, and chariots everywhere. He panics and cries out to his master, the prophet Elisha, "What will we do now?" Elisha reassures him not to worry, but the servant is still quite frightened. Elisha then prays for God to "open his eyes and let him see!" The servant is amazed to observe a mighty angelic force of horses and chariots of fire between himself and the enemy. (See 2 Kings 6:15-17.) We all need God to help us to see.

One of the most effective ways to open our spiritual eyes is through prayer. Without prayer, our spirits shrivel and die. Mother Teresa said, "Prayer is putting oneself in the hands of God." Martin Luther said that "prayer is the mightiest of all weapons that created natures can wield." Prayer is our connection to and communication with God. It is powerful not because of anything we do but because of who God is. It has such great significance in this universe because God listens, is touched, and chooses to respond to our stumbling words.

Prayer is our lifeline to God and to reality. In many ways, it is the secret to opening our spiritual eyes, meeting our spiritual needs, and energizing our spiritual passions. Prayer is a necessity to our spirits, just as air is a necessity to our bodies. Because of this, the more we pray, the stronger, the healthier, and the more balanced we can be.

The brilliant writer G. K. Chesterton wrote, "You say grace before meals. All right. But I say grace before the concert and the opera, and grace before the play and pantomime, and grace before I open a book, and grace before sketching, painting, swimming, fencing, boxing, walking, playing, dancing, and grace before I dip the pen in the ink."

Another way to open our spiritual eyes and nurture our spirits is what Brother Lawrence called "the practice of the presence of God." Brother Lawrence washed pots and pans in a monastery in Paris during the seventeenth century. His desire was to foster an awareness of God's closeness in the midst of every simple act he did—whether it was making an omelet, sweeping the floor, or serving breakfast to his colleagues. Brother Lawrence found God everywhere and acknowledged that presence without interruption. His close friend Joseph de Beaufort wrote, "Brother Lawrence insisted that, to be constantly aware of God's presence, it is necessary to form the habit of continually talking with Him throughout the day. To think that we must abandon conversation with Him in order to deal with the world is erroneous. Instead, as we nourish our souls by seeing God in His exaltation, we will derive a great joy at being His." Therefore, set reminders throughout your everyday life—

when you wash a dish or stop at a red light or get a phone call—that become triggers to think about God and be more fully aware of his presence.

Brother Lawrence definitely knew how to take care of his spirit. We all need to cry out with David, "Renew a loyal spirit within me" (Psalm 51:10). Prayer and practicing the presence of God will certainly set you on the right path to spiritual balance.

Balance is hard to define, but you know when you have it. More accurately, you know when you've lost it. When you've lost your balance

- your mind can't think right

- your heart feels out of control

- your relationships grow painful

- your body trips or falls

- your spirit seems distant from God

Balance is the key to growth. When your life is balanced, you'll have better perspective, more peace, and a sense of purpose. It's these things that will help you stay above the drama that often plays out in your everyday activities.

TODAY'S TOOLS

Prayer

Dear God,

Thank you for caring enough to walk through all the challenges and difficulties of this life with me.

Help me to renew my mind and clean up my thoughts. Forgive me for the times I have allowed my thoughts to stray into areas I know they should never go. Fill me with your thoughts.

Soften my heart and give me your precious peace. When destructive emotions drag me down, please hear my voice as I cry out to you. Forgive me when my emotions lead me into sin.

Empower me to move beyond self-absorption to a place where I may love others as you love me. Build in me your plan and pattern for relationships through connection, care, concern, comfort, communication, celebration, and the creation of community.

Strengthen my body. Protect it from disease and accident. Remind me daily that it is the temple of the Holy Spirit, and motivate me to treat it as you would wish.

Teach me to pray—really pray—knowing you are listening intently to my every word. Open my eyes to the spiritual universe that surrounds me. Make me aware of your presence each moment of every day.

Amen.

Passage

Be very careful, then, how you live—not as unwise but as wise, making the most of every opportunity.
Ephesians 5:15-16 (NIV)

Practice

① Which of the five arms of balance are you weakest in? Reread that section of the chapter, highlighting ideas that might help you strengthen that area in your life.

② Circle the emotions below that best describe your most difficult day in the past month.

Anger	Exhaustion	Loneliness
Anxiety	Fear	Resentment
Bitterness	Humiliation	Sadness
Confusion	Hurt	Uneasiness
Depression	Jealousy	

Talk to a friend about these emotions. Together come up with some ways to help you to deal with these difficult feelings.

③ Commit to practicing the presence of God for one full day this week.

RULE ❺
LET GO

IT HAD BEEN a long and dangerous journey.

Frodo's mission was to carry the Ring of Power to Mount Doom in Mordor, where it could be destroyed. Now he stands, along with his trusted companion, Sam, at the edge of the fiery abyss. But he hesitates, battling with himself about throwing the ring into the flames.

"What are you waiting for?" Sam cries out to Frodo in the 2003 movie *The Return of the King*. "Just let it go."

Still Frodo struggles. He knows Sam is right, but with the alluring ring in his hand, it doesn't seem that simple. It takes a deadly attack from Gollum to wrench the ring from Frodo's grasp. Finally the ring is destroyed, and everybody watching the movie sighs. In the book of the same title, J. R. R. Tolkien describes how Frodo was affected by letting go of the ring: "In his eyes there was peace now. . . . His burden was taken away. . . . He was himself again, he was free."

Holding on to certain things can hurt you. They can

- distort your mind
- harden your heart

- push away your relationships

- damage your body

- block your spirit

As Frodo discovered, things that seem small can bring a big burden. Frequently we don't fully understand how large the burden is until we let it go.

I don't like taking out the trash. But whenever the garbage can under the sink gets full, I take it to the big can in the garage. Then every Tuesday night I wheel the big can out to the curb. If I decided not to take out the trash for a month or two, garbage would pile up and a distinct odor would permeate my house. Letting go is like taking out the garbage. Every day there are at least three things we all need to regularly consider letting go of: anger, worry, and material possessions.

ANGER

Anger is dangerous. It can destroy you and those around you. It can destroy marriages, families, friendships, and jobs. Solomon said, "Fools vent their anger" (Proverbs 29:11). The book of Proverbs also says that unmanaged anger leads to restlessness and foolishness, creates quarrels, alienates those we love, and steals our peace.

Anger happens when we have unmet expectations—when we believe we deserve certain things but those things don't happen the way we think they should. We get angry when we believe that we must succeed at all we do, that others must meet our criteria of behavior, or that we deserve to be treated a certain way. Unrealistic expectations get us nowhere except more upset. This anger isn't worth holding on to. Here are six steps to letting go:

① **Admit your emotions.** If you're angry, be honest with yourself about it. Don't deny it, ignore it, or bury it.

② **Calm down.** If your anger is getting out of control, lower your voice, sit down, and breathe deeply. If you still can't calm down, remove yourself from the situation.

③ **Work out your anger.** Physical activity can reduce your anger. Go for a drive, weed a garden, paint a room, write a letter, or take a long walk.

④ **Talk about your anger.** Take responsibility for your feelings. Be direct and honest without blaming or attacking. The better you can communicate about your anger, the more you can control it.

⑤ **Don't let the sun go down on your anger.** Resolve your anger as soon as possible. Unresolved anger is extremely destructive. The sooner you handle your anger, the better.

⑥ **Give it to God.** The ultimate solution to every problem is God. Give your anger to him each day and let him take care of it. He will never let you down.

Do as many of these as are helpful. Letting go isn't always instantaneous, but it is well worth whatever time it takes. So "get rid of all bitterness, rage, anger, harsh words, and slander, as well as all types of evil behavior. Instead, be kind to each other, tenderhearted, forgiving one another, just as God through Christ has forgiven you" (Ephesians 4:31-32).

WORRY

Some people are like turtles—most worries just roll off their backs. Others are like sponges—they soak up worries, and over time they sour. Certain people worry more than others, but we all tend to worry about something. It may be money, safety, our appearance, our performance, friends, family, love, or a thousand other things. Worry accomplishes nothing positive. Paul J. Meyer wrote, "It is a downward spiral. . . . It lets the air out of all you do, draining the fun and excitement from everything."

Worry makes us irritable or impatient or negative. It can keep you up at night or make your stomach ache. It can make it hard to concentrate and make you so forgetful you think you have Alzheimer's. Worry can be so overwhelming that it leads to severe stress, panic attacks, phobias, or a number of other anxiety disorders. It's a terrible habit and an incredible waste of time. The more you worry, the less you accomplish. As Mark Twain wrote, "I am an old man and I have known a great many troubles, but most of them have never happened." In the Sermon on the Mount, Jesus said there are two things we need not worry about: today and tomorrow (see Matthew 6:25, 34). In my thinking, that covers just about everything. We don't need to worry about today—God will take care of it. We don't need to worry about tomorrow—it's already in his hands. So let go of all your worries. I wonder if the apostle Peter was reflecting on Jesus' words when he wrote, "Give all your worries and cares to God, for he cares about you" (1 Peter 5:7).

My good friend Pam Vredevelt has written a practical little book entitled *Letting Go of Worry and Anxiety*, which includes many ways to deal with your worries. Here are four of them:

Review the facts. Focus your attention on what is, not on what if. A mind that feeds on the facts is less likely to fall prey to a frenzied imagination that casts illusions as reality.

Reconnect with the present. Many of our worries stem from a tendency to overestimate the probability of a harmful event and to exaggerate its potential negative effect.

Refuse to assume the worst. A concern is a concern, not a major disaster. A temporary setback is just that, not a permanent failure cast in stone for all eternity. Keep that in mind the next time you start to assume the worst.

Rely on faith. Let's allow our anxieties to be a reminder to surrender ourselves fully to God in trust and humility. Let's use worry to trigger a prayer.

MATERIAL POSSESSIONS

Most of us have way too much stuff. It clutters our lives, but we still dream of new, more exciting possessions. Many of us collect something—clothes, cars, art, trading cards, music, movies, and on and on. We treasure our special things. Stuff may be attractive, but it rarely satisfies for long. I frequently feel overwhelmed by all the stuff in my house. The problem isn't just that it seems to grow but that it requires care and repair. It must be stored and organized and protected. It often owns us as much as we own it. We love our stuff, but it is an addictive trap.

Jesus tells us not to "store up treasures here on earth" where nothing lasts. Rather, "store your treasures in heaven," because "wherever your treasure is, there the desires of your heart will also be" (Matthew 6:19-21). We are like children building sand castles on the seashore, naively thinking that they are strong and indestructible and that the ocean's waves will never touch them. Yet what we build and collect here on earth fades so quickly. The waves come, and our castles collapse and are washed away. Within a few minutes we can't even find the place where our beautiful castle once stood so proudly. Possessions don't last. As Randy Alcorn wrote in *The Treasure Principle*, "The more you have, the more you'll leave behind."

Dr. Billy Graham tells the story of a little boy who got his hand stuck inside a valuable vase. His father patiently tried to help the boy remove his hand, but it wouldn't come out. The father was thinking of breaking the vase when he said, "Now, my son, make one more try. Open your hand, and hold your fingers out straight and then pull." To his astonishment, the little fellow said, "Oh no, Father. I couldn't put my fingers out like that, because if I did I would drop my penny."

Dr. Graham finishes his story by saying, "Smile if you will—but thousands of us are like that little boy, so busy holding on to the world's worthless penny that we cannot accept liberation. I beg you to drop that trifle in your heart. Surrender! Let go, and let God have his way in your life."

To let go is to admit we can't control everything. To let go is to recognize that anger rarely gets us what we want. To let go is to give all our worries to him who has power over each today and every tomorrow. To let go is to realize that missionary Jim Elliot was right when he said, "He is no fool who gives what he cannot keep to gain what he cannot lose." To let go is to live each day to the fullest.

TODAY'S TOOLS

Prayer

Dear God,

Thank you that your beloved Son let go of his place in heaven to come live as a man on this planet.

Teach me how to let go of all the hurts and regrets of my past. Point me forward to the incredible future you have planned specifically for me.

Help me to be angry only at the things that make you angry. And when I am angry, show me how to express it in a good and godly way.

Cleanse me from all worry, replacing it with deep trust in you. When the fears and concerns of this world surround me, draw me closer to you.

Create in me a heart and mind that is not owned by stuff. Remind me daily that the treasures of heaven put the treasures of earth to shame.

Show me anything that I need to let go of: pride, unhealthy attitudes, bad habits, prejudices, insecurities. Forgive me for not letting go when I know I should. As I trust you by releasing my hold, fill me with your peace and joy and freedom.

Amen.

Passage

You were taught . . . to put off your old self, which is being corrupted by its deceitful desires . . . and to put on the new self, created to be like God in true righteousness and holiness.
Ephesians 4:22, 24 (NIV)

Practice

① Of the six steps to letting go of anger on page 45, circle the ones that are the most difficult for you. Share them with a close friend and discuss how you might work through them.

② What are your top three worries? What do you need to do to break the habit of worrying?

③ Adopt one of the following ideas to help you let go of "stuff."

> *Whenever you purchase something new, discard one old item.*

> *Hold a yearly garage sale.*

> *Lend your things liberally to others.*

> *Give things away to those who have a need.*

> *Declutter your home, donating extra items to charity.*

> *Consider carefully all nonessential purchases.*

> *Shop only when you have a specific need.*

RULE ❻
REACH OUT

THE OLD MAN lived by the sea. Each day when the tide went out, he would slowly, meticulously walk along the rocky shore. Every once in a while he bent down, picked up a starfish that had been stranded by the retreating ocean and probably would die before the tide returned, and threw it back into the sea. One day a neighbor who had frequently watched the old man's routine called out, "Hey, what are you doing? Don't you know that this beach goes on for hundreds of miles and that thousands of starfish get washed up on it every day? Surely you don't think that throwing a few back is going to matter!"

The old man paused with a smile, then held up the starfish in his hand. "It matters to this one," he said.

Every person matters.

Every person we meet has incredible value. Yet it is so easy to walk by them without any sense of how unique and talented and full of incredible potential they are. All we need to do is reach out, but we hesitate. We don't have the time or the interest or the confidence. We leave it to somebody else. In his book *Locking Arms*, Stu Weber challenges each of us to step forward. "You be the one to reach out. You be the one to start the conversation. . . . Look people in the eye, learn names, study hearts. And reach out."

Reaching out does much more than impact others; it changes and enriches who you are. Each day, try to reach out in these five ways.

NOTICE

Every day can be so full and busy that it feels overwhelming. We skim across the surface of life, hardly even noticing the people we pass by. We have perfected the art of seeing without noticing. In Thornton Wilder's play *Our Town*, Emily cries out, "Oh, Mama, just look at me one minute as though you really saw me. . . . Let's look at each other." In frustration she gives up trying to get people to really notice each other and concludes that we are all just blind to those around us. We frequently have eyes that don't truly see and ears that don't seem to hear. As a result, we don't reach out to those around us who need a little compassion. Saint Augustine said that we all need hands to help others, feet to hasten to those in need, eyes to see misery and want, and ears to hear the sighs and sorrows of those around us.

I once visited a church that was mourning the suicide of a bright and beautiful sixteen-year-old girl. The people were in shock, unable to absorb the tragedy of it all. But the hardest thing to face was her suicide note. The last lines went something like this: "My struggles felt too big and too hard. I tried my best to cry out for help, but nobody seemed to notice." Over the years those last four words have haunted me: *nobody seemed to notice.*

So please look around and notice. Please don't let the words of that sixteen-year-old refer to you.

WELCOME AND ACCEPT

I love a warm welcome. When it is clear someone is glad to see you, he or she makes you feel wanted. The person smiles and asks you all sorts of questions, actually listening to your answers without interrupting. He or she might even ask you to stay for dinner. Then when you must leave, the host appears genuinely sad that your time together has come to an end. Too often when I call someone or drop by that person's home, I feel as if I've interrupted something and that I'm an intruder. The person wishes to be polite, but he or she doesn't have the time to reach out. With places to go and things to do, the person seems to be trying to get rid of me in order to move on with life.

The apostle Peter reminds us to "cheerfully share your home with those who need a meal or a place to stay" (1 Peter 4:9). Most of us yearn for a slower pace so we can really connect with others, but we don't do anything to foster such a world. We don't have the time for hospitality, even though our souls ache for it. Hospitality requires breaking through the tendencies of isolation, detachment, independence, self-protection, and self-absorption. It requires reaching out, and its rewards are incredible. What you gain through hospitality is so much more than what you give. At its core, hospitality means to welcome and accept. Paul put it simply: "Practice hospitality" (Romans 12:13, NIV). The Greek word that he uses here encompasses two specific elements: to act as a friend and to act as a host. I encourage you to reach out daily to be both of these. My friend Pastor Doug Hiebenthal wrote that hospitality requires

- including others in your plans and activities

- setting time aside to make connections with new people

- making room for people at your table, in your home, and in your life

- helping people feel included, accepted, and more comfortable

- sharing what you have with others

- moving beyond your present friends to include new friends

- being purposeful in your use of time with others outside your comfort zone

- responding to others by design and not default

Integrating these values into our lives will enrich us in surprising ways. The writer of Hebrews said, "Don't forget to show hospitality to strangers, for some who have done this have entertained angels without realizing it!" (Hebrews 13:2).

To welcome others involves accepting them. You need not agree with them or be attracted to them, but you can still reach out and accept them. Paul tells us to "accept one another" (Romans 15:7, NIV). Why? Because Jesus accepted you.

LISTEN

It is amazing how much we can learn by keeping quiet and listening. It is also one of the most effective ways to reach out to others. Paul Tournier wrote in *To Understand Each Other* that it is impossible to overemphasize the immense need people have to be really listened to. It affirms them. It shows we care and exhibits respect. Sometimes a silent mouth and an attentive ear are the most loving things we can offer.

Everybody wants to be heard. Sometimes just by listening to someone we can help that person

- clarify thinking

- reduce stress

- build confidence

- experience hope

- feel love

Listening takes discipline as we stop what we're doing and focus on the other person's words, meanings, emotions, and concerns. Listening says, "You are important." It reaches out by taking an interest in someone else's journey and wanting to know his or her story. When we place our focus on others instead of ourselves, our worries and difficulties seem to shrink. Listening builds character.

ENCOURAGE AND AFFIRM

Life can be hard. Some days we feel lonely, frustrated, worn out, rejected, used, depressed, unappreciated, or hopeless. These are the times we need someone to reach out and come alongside us. Billy Graham wrote, "There are so many hurts that circumstances and the world inflict upon us, we need the constant reinforcement of encouragement."

A good friend of mine was at the grocery store when she felt God nudge her to buy two bouquets of bright spring flowers. So she got one for herself and one to encourage someone else. On the way out of the store, she saw an elderly woman who appeared distraught. My friend walked up to her, handed her a bouquet, and said, "This is for you. Have a great day." A smile crossed the woman's face as she replied, "Oh, thank you. Today is my wedding anniversary, but my husband has passed away. He always gave me flowers on this day." My friend had no idea how encouraging her little gift was going to be.

A little encouragement can make a big difference in a person's life. We all need encouragement. Yet the world is full of discouragers. It is easier to ignore, criticize, control, or lecture than it is to reach out and encourage. Discouragement focuses on the negative, while encouragement builds up the positive.

As a psychologist, I've observed over and over again that people become what you encourage them to be. I challenge you to expose people's strengths and cover their weaknesses. Be liberal with your praise. Mother Teresa said, "Kind words can be short and easy to speak, but their echoes are truly endless."

PRAY

Prayer is an incredible tool. It involves bringing people before God and asking him to provide protection, direction, and blessings. I used to pray quietly for people without ever letting them know what I was doing. Now I'm bolder about it, and I ask, "May I pray for you?" "What do I need to know that would help me pray best for you?" or "Would you like to pray together?" As I've asked these questions, not one person has been offended or turned down my offer of prayer.

Frequently, reaching out means taking a risk. So I'd like to encourage you to pray for people who may be outside your comfort zone. Pray for the weak and disconnected—the challenged, the lonely, the hurting, and the struggling people of your world. Pray for your enemies—those who hurt you or hate you or harm you, those who anger you or disgust you or cause you to feel uncomfortable. Pray for the lost and confused—those who are thirsty for love and acceptance, security and recognition. They are like us in more ways than we really wish to admit.

Pray for the people on the fringes of your life—the person who delivers your mail, works at your local gas station, checks your groceries, picks up your garbage, and all the others who live in the shadows of your life. Pray for the strangers—those you don't know and have never met, someone you've heard about or read about, a friend of a friend, a neighbor, anyone new to reach out to. As you reach out to pray for individuals in each of these categories, remember the words of Samuel Taylor Coleridge: "He prayeth best who loveth best."

FORMS OF LOVE

All five of these means of reaching out are forms of love. In love we give our time and attention, our encouragement and prayers. Ruth Stafford Peale said it so simply: "Find a need and fill it." The world is full of people with needs, both great and small. As you reach out and attempt to meet some of those needs, you can be assured that you are changing your own world in a positive way. Winston Churchill said, "What is the use of living, if it not be to strive for noble causes to make this muddled world a better place?" How beautiful and inspiring to hear stories of people giving to each other. Reaching out is an act of giving—we give patience, respect, and grace. Reaching out must be more than an activity or a hobby or a good deed. It must be an act of giving yourself and an act of love.

Every year thousands of people from all over the world come together for the Special Olympics. It is an exciting event in which disabled athletes give their best in joyful competition of sports and determination. A number of years ago, five young runners stood at the starting line. They crouched into position, and the starter's gun fired. The five burst onto the track and were running with all they could give. It was a close race, with each athlete pushing to his limit and the crowd cheering them on.

Suddenly one of the runners tripped and fell flat on his face. He tried to pull himself to his feet, but he was dazed since the wind had been knocked out of him. The crowd gasped, and some shook their heads in sadness, knowing the disappointment of the young runner. But in the next moment a surprise overtook the crowd. Another athlete stopped running, went back, and reached out to help the fallen boy to his feet. The two of them finished the race together, and the people stood to their feet, cheering them on.

That is love. That is what reaching out is all about.

TODAY'S TOOLS

Prayer

Dear God,
Thank you for taking the time to reach out to me when you are so great and I am so small. Thank you for bringing people into my life at key moments when I am lonely, confused, discouraged, or in need of help.

Stretch me out of my comfort zone and beyond my selfishness. Teach me that every person has great worth and surprising potential. Forgive me for failing to reach out to the people in my world as you would. Forgive me for all the times I failed to notice them, welcome and accept them, listen to them, encourage and affirm them, and even pray for them.

Remind me to pray hard and sincerely for those in need. Give me compassion for all who are struggling, even if they are enemies or people I hardly know. Use me to help bring them closer to you.

Give me the courage to reach out to someone each and every day. Show me what to do and tell me what to say. Build in my heart a true love for all those you bring into my life.

Amen.

Passage

The whole law can be summed up in this one command: "Love your neighbor as yourself."
Galatians 5:14

Practice

① Carl Sandburg once said that *exclusive* is the ugliest word in the English language. Is there someone you have excluded by failing to reach out? If so, what might you do to change this situation?

② Invite people you don't know well to your house for dinner. Greet them warmly and proactively to help them feel as if your home is their home.

③ Make it a goal to encourage one person every day for the next month. This can be done through:

> *a smile*
>
> *a positive attitude*
>
> *a compliment*
>
> *a gift*
>
> *a helping hand*
>
> *a listening ear*
>
> *a hug*
>
> *a note or a card*

④ Consider someone on the fringes of your life and commit to pray for that person regularly for one month.

RULE ❼
CELEBRATE

JOYCE FELT LIKE a modern-day Job.

In the past year, her husband of twenty-five years had died of a sudden heart attack, she had lost her job because of downsizing, her teenage daughter had gotten into a serious car accident, and now her house was going into foreclosure because she couldn't make the payments. Joyce sat in my office and wept. I wept with her. I wondered, *How can I encourage this woman when her situation seems so overwhelming?*

But then Joyce surprised me. She wiped her tears and said, "Life is hard, but God is good."

"Excuse me?" I said.

"Life is hard," she repeated, "but God is good. I know that somehow he's going to take care of me and the kids. I just want to celebrate that my daughter is alive and that I am healthy and that I have met some of the most wonderful, supportive people ever during the past year."

Celebrate? My mind reeled. *Did she just say* celebrate? *How can a woman in her situation celebrate?*

After she left, I was struck with the following statement from the beginning of the book of James: "When troubles come your way, consider it an opportunity for great joy" (James 1:2).

We all need to celebrate in both good times and bad. Every day I want to find something to celebrate. Some people find joy easy to grasp. They naturally celebrate every opportunity they get. Others find it as elusive as the pot of gold at the end of a rainbow. They feel that joy has been hidden, and no matter how long they look, it stays beyond their grasp.

Medical conditions, depression, loss, anxiety, and failure are just a few of the things that can make joy seem distant. Yet regardless of how elusive joy is, "a cheerful heart is good medicine" (Proverbs 17:22). Celebration decreases our blood pressure, boosts our immune system, and makes us feel better. It enriches our perspective on life, energizes our spirits, and gives us fulfillment. So we must take celebration seriously. How can we embrace joy every day?

Someone once said that "cheerfulness greases the axles of the world." It energizes us and brightens up our world. It makes us want to dance and celebrate. Life is full of things that make us want to leap for joy. No healthy person would deny the power of love. Literature, movies, and music are full of romantic images. Love makes us want to celebrate. After more than twenty years of marriage to my wife, Tami, I'm still filled with an indescribable joy when I hear a special song or feel her gentle kiss.

It's the same type of feeling I get when I remember the day each of our children was born. The first cry, the tiny hands and feet, the helpless dependence, the incredible potential—these miraculous moments are imprinted on my soul and give me unlimited appreciation for life.

Every day we are surrounded by hundreds of reasons to celebrate. To have a great day, we must let these joys fill our hearts by being constantly aware of joy and nurturing it daily. Rejoice in the intricacies of a spiderweb, applaud the courage of a child learning to walk, feel the thrill of a well-run race, delight in the words that perfectly capture the moment. As you rejoice in these little things, you will show the world the amazing strength of simple celebration. Let's look at four wonderful expressions of joy.

SMILE

An old Japanese proverb says, "Fortune comes to those who smile." In fact, Charles Schwab, the first president of U.S. Steel, once said that his smile was worth a million dollars. We are drawn to people who smile. They make us feel relaxed and accepted. I want to spend time with people who smile because they bring out the smile in me. Dale Carnegie wrote in his classic *How to Win Friends and Influence People* that "a smile says, 'I like you. You make me happy. I am glad to see you.'"

A simple smile has great power. I was walking down the sidewalk on a sunny spring morning when I passed a grumpy-looking woman. I was smiling, and I gave her a friendly nod. "Excuse me," she said, "why are you smiling?" I stopped and responded, "It's such a beautiful morning that I can't stop myself." The lady thought about that for a moment and said, "I think I like you." As she walked away, a slight smile began to cross her face.

A smile is a wonderful gift to give others and yourself. So greet anybody you meet with a warm smile. Frank Fletcher once wrote that a simple smile "is rest to the weary, daylight to the discouraged, sunshine to the sad, and nature's best antidote for trouble." But not only does a smile do good to others, it does good to you. It improves your attitude, lifts your spirit, and makes you feel good. No matter what your situation, if you smile, it helps you feel better. And if others see it, they feel better too. King Solomon summed this up by simply saying, "A cheerful look brings joy to the heart" (Proverbs 15:30).

LAUGH

I love to laugh. There is something freeing about laughter, something that makes all of life seem more joyful. An old French saying insists that "the most completely lost of all days is the one on which I have not laughed." A smile touches your heart, but a laugh touches your whole body. I feel sad for the person who doesn't laugh frequently. To lose the power to laugh is to lose the power to enjoy life. So laugh every chance you get, and share your laughter with others. As Thomas Moore prayed, "Lord, give me a sense of humor that I may take some happiness from this life and share it with others."

Healthy people laugh. They have learned the great benefits of letting laughter flow. Here are a few of those benefits:

- **It is contagious.** When you laugh, so do others.

- **It blocks depression.** It is hard to laugh and be depressed simultaneously.

- **It reduces stress.** A good laugh distracts you from your worries.

- **It attracts others.** People are drawn to a hearty laugh.

- **It makes difficult situations tolerable.** A laugh lightens even the heaviest load.

Find something funny and allow yourself a good, long laugh. For, as Tim Hansel wrote, "He who laughs . . . lasts."

PLAY

My two sons are constantly asking me, "Dad will you play with us?" They love to play LEGOs, soccer, basketball, video games, and army men. It's easy to come up with great excuses not to play. There are chores to do and places to go. I'm too tired, too busy, too mature. But what if playing is the most important thing you do all day? Children know how to play and have fun; they smile and laugh and have a great time. Adults should follow their example a little more often. Antoine de Saint-Exupéry wrote, "All grown-ups were once children—although few of them remember it." We get too distracted by the serious side of life. We need to develop a playfulness that holds its own against all the cares and concerns that overwhelm us.

Play helps us to lighten up. It relaxes us and brings us joy. Without play we become grumpy old killjoys who stifle our own ability to have fun and freedom. We become worn-out control freaks who make others uptight and fearful. Therefore, when friends or children or anybody else asks you to play, welcome the opportunity.

GET EXCITED

Every day is full of excitement, and this excitement should be celebrated. We fail to let joy touch our emotions and get us energized and enthusiastic. We let ourselves become subdued and bored; we tiptoe through our days without diving in and celebrating how amazing it all is. I want to get excited about every sunrise or sunset I view, every breath I take, every person I meet, and every challenge I encounter!

If I allow myself this type of excitement, my joy becomes unstoppable. I enjoy passionate people—those who have discovered a passion and are enthusiastic about it. If you struggle in this area, commit yourself to *finding your passion*. Ask yourself questions such as, *What energizes me? What do I do well? What am I drawn to when I'm bored?* These questions get you started on an amazing journey. A passion is different for each person. For one, it might be an athletic activity; for another, it's working with kids or gardening or writing. Once you think you have found it, *feed your passion*. Explore it, practice it, research it. Spend time and energy developing it. A passion that is not fed can easily wither and die. I encourage you to *fulfill your passion*. It doesn't have to be your full-time or even part-time job. It may be something you do with your free time. However you fit it into your life, set goals and dreams involving your passion. Goals move you forward, stretch you, and help you turn your dreams into reality. A life without dreams is often drained of joy. Dreams add excitement, and excitement leads to celebration.

Life is hard. We are surrounded by difficulties, but we still have plenty of opportunities for celebration. Even if the night is dark, joy will come in the morning. Faith involves believing that there is a reason to celebrate, even when the feelings and circumstances don't point in that direction. As G. K. Chesterton wrote, "Joy is the gigantic secret of the Christian." Yet it must be chosen, pursued, and requested. For some it may come quickly and with little effort. For others the journey is long and the effort exhausting. But whoever you are and wherever you may be, my prayer for you is the same as Paul's: "May the God of hope fill you with all joy and peace" (Romans 15:13, NIV).

TODAY'S TOOLS

Prayer

Dear God,

You are a God of joy and gladness—the Lord of celebration. So help me to celebrate. Help me to rejoice, even when life is hard, my energy is low, and my emotions are flat.

Open my eyes and ears to all the joy around me. Forgive me for not allowing the wonders of your world to touch my heart and uplift my spirit.

Show me your smile. Bring me laughter. Teach me to play. Touch me with the incredible excitement of who you are and what you desire for me.

Fill me with gladness every morning, and let it build throughout the day. Thank you for your amazing love and all the joy it gives. Let me so overflow with your joy that it brightens the lives of everyone I meet.

Amen.

Passage

Always be full of joy in the Lord.
Philippians 4:4

Practice

① Commit yourself to a day of smiles. When you first wake up, smile for one minute, then smile at every person you meet for the rest of the day.

② Make a list of at least five things you have been excited about in the past. Then add five things you might get excited about today.

③ Throw a party! Find an excuse, any excuse, to celebrate. Sometime in the next two weeks, gather together friends or family, serve food, play games, laugh, and have fun.

RULE ⓼
DIG DEEP

"YOU'VE GOT TO DIG DEEPER."

"But isn't this deep enough?"

"Not yet," Dad said. "Put your weight into it. You can go a little deeper."

I can still remember the sweat rolling off my forehead as I dug fence-post holes with my father. The ground was hard, and at times we'd hit a rock. I'd get tired, and he'd simply say, "Dig deeper."

Later I found that if your post was too shallow, it would become wobbly and maybe even lean to one side or the other. Yet if the post was set deep enough, it would stand strong and straight.

I think this is also true of people. If we dig deep—search for knowledge and work to broaden our outlook—we will stand strong and straight. This is an important means to gain the abundant life. However, this task is not easy. Rick Warren wrote, "There are no shortcuts to maturity." The ground is often hard, and our muscles grow tired. But if we are persistent, the rewards are great.

If we're willing to dig deep, we must be willing to go beyond our own superficiality. We have all grown shallow. William James wrote that "compared to what we ought to be, we are only half awake. . . . We are making use of only a small part of our possible mental and physical resources. . . . The human individual thus lives far within his limits; he possesses powers of various sorts which he habitually fails to use." We skate on the surface of life, racing through experiences without truly experiencing them. We rarely dig deep. As Richard Foster said, "Superficiality is the curse of our age." There are at least five basic principles that will lead us to depth and maturity.

COMMIT YOURSELF TO LEARNING

Learning is open to everyone, regardless of age, wealth, social status, or intelligence. The only requirement is that we are teachable, for learning requires an attitude that says, "I'm a student, and I want to know more." This process is active; we must search for it and work for it. Learning isn't always easy; it challenges us by making us think and feel and sometimes even change. This can be exciting and exhilarating, but it can also be uncomfortable. Learning will question and convict. It can cut deeply into your beliefs and prejudices, forcing you to rethink and relearn what you once took for granted. Learning allows you to know more but makes you realize how little you truly understand. It also moves you to action—to apply what you have learned and to reach out with that learning to those around you.

I recently met a delightful couple in their mid-eighties. They were intelligent, articulate, and had an insatiable curiosity. We had a wonderful discussion about everything from current events to geography, theology, movies, and engineering. After a while I asked, "What is your secret to such great conversation?" The wife laughed and said, "It's simple; we are lifelong learners. We are students at the university." The husband added, "Learning keeps the mind awake." Lifelong learning is a key to growth, for there is always more to learn. Harvey Ullman wrote that "anyone who stops learning is old, whether this happens at twenty or eighty." Likewise, digging deep and being lifelong learners keeps us young, even if we are eighty-six or older.

READ WIDELY

The world is full of incredible ideas, mind-expanding thoughts, and interesting experiences. Reading opens us up to all of these. In their enjoyable little book God Is in the Small Stuff, Bruce Bickel and Stan Jantz wrote, "Reading is the gateway for growth. Books contain information, insight and inspiration—all of which contribute significantly to your mental and spiritual development. . . . Good books also present ideas and concepts that stretch beyond our self-imposed limits." Therefore, dig deep by reading a broad diversity of books, authors, and topics. Try to avoid the trap of reading only those books that reinforce what you already believe.

I love lists. Over the years I have collected a number of book lists, such as The 100 Best Books of All Time, The Most Influential Books of the Twentieth Century, and The Books Every Christian Should Read. I want to read books that have had a significant impact on others. In *A Severe Mercy*, Sheldon Vanauken relates an agreement between him and his wife that if either one found a book to be meaningful, the other would read it too. By so doing, they drew closer and discovered a faith that changed their lives.

Finding good and powerful books can be a challenge, but thousands exist. Every time I visit with my brother-in-law, Todd, he asks me sometime in our conversation, "What good books have you read lately?" If I give him a title, he will pull out a piece of paper from his wallet and write it down. Todd knows the importance of reading widely.

Find a good book today and jump into it, even if it is just for a few minutes. If you don't have a good book, ask a friend for a recommendation. Or visit a library or browse a bookstore. Henry Ward Beecher wrote, "A book is . . . a garden, an orchard, a storehouse, a party, a company . . . a multitude of counselors." Reading can deepen your day.

ASK QUESTIONS

You cannot dig deep without asking questions. Bill Mowry wrote, "Learners ask good questions. They possess an insatiable curiosity—a longing to know, discover, and inquire." Yet many people are hesitant to ask. Maybe they believe they should already know the answers, or they are afraid they might sound foolish. Others don't want to pry or interrupt. So they keep their questions locked away, missing real opportunities to learn and dig deep. The solution is simple—just ask. There is nothing wrong, foolish, or inappropriate about an honest question born out of pure motives.

Questions are amazing tools that allow us to get to the heart of an issue or a person. As a psychologist, I ask hundreds of questions of every client I meet. People are usually surprised at how much they open up and what they share in fifty minutes of therapy. But I just ask and listen. The power of a simple question is something we all need to explore. Questions can

- open up new doors

- lead to understanding

- break through superficiality

- clarify confusion

- communicate caring

- correct misinformation

- reinforce possibilities

- satisfy curiosity

Questions are crucial to your growth and ability to dig deep. So ask questions of yourself and others. With everyone you meet—whether a close friend, a complete stranger, or anyone in between—be prepared with a few questions. Once you get started, who knows where you might end up?

EXPLORE NEW IDEAS

Too often we get stuck in the rut of what is comfortable and familiar. New thoughts might force us to reconsider our beliefs and prejudices, and that feels far too threatening. So we close our minds and thus stop growing. Will Henry said that "an open mind collects more riches than an open purse." A closed mind collects nothing and often goes bankrupt. An open mind is alive and flexible and capable of seeing any situation from a multitude of perspectives. It has the freedom to rethink its positions and reevaluate its opinions. William Blake wrote that "the man who never alters his opinion is like standing water, and breeds reptiles of the mind." I wonder if a lot of us have grown stagnant and need some fresh ideas to clean out our thinking. So what gets us so stuck? Why don't we grow? Here are a few reasons:

- We have a lot to unlearn.

- We are too comfortable.

- We are afraid.

- We don't want to upset people.

- We are easily distracted.

- We are too overwhelmed.

To dig deep is to grow in spite of any of these reasons. It's to face the new with excitement and not let our preconceived notions imprison us. It's to realize that we might not know the answer to every question and to understand that the answers we have held on to so firmly might be incomplete, inaccurate, or imperfect. So I awake each morning wondering what I will discover today. I love the way Samuel Johnson put it: "The world is not yet exhausted; let me see something tomorrow which I never saw before."

SEEK COUNSEL

You can't dig deep without the help of others. We all need guides—people who have gone before us and know the way. People who are committed to learning can direct us to good books, assist us with probing questions, and present new ideas. Sometimes parents or pastors can fill this role. Other times we need a mentor, coach, spiritual director, counselor, or group. King Solomon was considered the wisest person in the world, but throughout Proverbs he wrote that the key to his success was seeking counsel. He said things such as, "Fools think their own way is right, but the wise listen to others," "Walk with the wise and become wise," "Get all the advice and instruction you can, so you will be wise the rest of your life," and "Plans succeed through good counsel" (Proverbs 12:15; 13:20; 19:20; 20:18). If King Solomon needed counsel, the rest of us really need it.

We all need to connect regularly with some type of coach. Yet we often see this as unnecessary or as a sign of weakness. We think we can do it on our own, and maybe we can, but why not learn from those who have gone before us? Andy Stanley said, "I can go farther and faster with someone coaching me than I can go on my own." I believe this is true of most of us. We all are too close to ourselves and our situations to be objective. We need others to help us work through our blind spots, insecurities, and weaknesses. James Belasco wrote, "Coaches help people grow. They help people see beyond what they are today to what they can become tomorrow."

Finding a coach starts with looking around you for people you respect—people who are wise or accomplished or skilled in areas you wish to pursue. In the Scriptures we find Moses mentoring Joshua, Eli teaching Samuel, Elijah being a role model for Elisha, and Paul guiding Timothy. Mentoring can happen formally or informally, individually or in a small group. The key is to be humble, teachable, and determined to become all God wants you to be.

My grandfather was a great coach. As a kid, I admired how he could do almost anything. He taught me how to tie my shoes, drive a tractor, and pan for gold. One day he grabbed a shovel and a gold pan, and the two of us walked down to Rough and Ready Creek. He explained that long ago the creek had shifted and left a vein of gold deep in the bank. So he forced his shovel into the sandy soil and reminded me, "You've got to dig deep." After digging awhile, he put some of the sand into my pan, and I dipped it into the creek. Then I swirled the water around and around in the pan until the lighter material was washed away. If I was patient and persistent, I would soon see a small streak of glitter at the bottom of my pan.

I learned some important lessons through this process, but the most important was that if you dig deep enough in the right spots and work your pan long enough, you will be amazed at the gold you can find in the most ordinary places.

TODAY'S TOOLS

Prayer

Dear God,

Thank you for surrounding me with so much to learn, so many wonderful books to read, so many fascinating questions to ask, so many new ideas to ponder, and so many capable people to meet.

Forgive me for all the times I don't dig deep into the opportunities you place before me. Forgive me for all the times fear or personal comfort or pride has kept me from growing.

Strengthen me so that I may go beyond the superficiality of the world. Give me the determination and persistence to try to understand as much as I can of your character, your Word, and your creation.

Show me books and questions and new ideas that will stretch me beyond my narrow boundaries and rigid prejudices.

Bring coaches, mentors, spiritual directors, and others into my life— those who can help me reach the potential you have placed in me.

Help me to dig deep so I may stand strong and straight. As I dig, show me your wisdom so I may live a life that is truly wise.

Amen.

Passage

Joyful is the person who finds wisdom, the one who gains understanding. For wisdom is more profitable than silver, and her wages are better than gold. Wisdom is more precious than rubies; nothing you desire can compare with her.

Proverbs 3:13-15

Practice

① Make a list of six books that would stretch you and help you grow. Commit to reading at least one book per month.

② Each morning, come up with a question you can ask that will help you get to know people you encounter. Make it a point to ask your question of at least three people every day.

③ What area of your life could you improve by having a coach? Consider someone who might be able to help you in this area. Ask that person to meet you for breakfast or lunch and discuss the idea of coaching.

RULE ❾
WORK HARD

PARALYZED FROM HEAD TO TOE.

A massive stroke imprisoned forty-three-year-old Jean-Dominique Bauby inside his own body, leaving him unable to speak or even move. With only his left eye functioning, he was able to communicate by blinking to select letters one at a time as a special alphabet was slowly recited to him. Through hard work, along with discipline and persistence, Jean-Dominique meticulously blinked out over sixteen thousand words to compose an amazing book. In *The Diving Bell and the Butterfly*, he artfully tells what's going on inside of him with observations that are both fascinating and emotionally charged.

To write a book is no easy task, but to write in Jean-Dominique's condition must have been incredibly demanding. Yet when the final letter of the final page was communicated, I bet he felt a rush of joy and satisfaction. Finishing a day of hard work feels so rewarding. We feel good, and we know it was somehow all worth it. Margaret Thatcher, former prime minister of Great Britain, wrote, "Look at a day when you are supremely satisfied at the end. It's not a day when you lounge around doing nothing; it's when you've had everything to do, and you've done it."

Many successful people praise the value of hard work. Charles Schwab, the first president of U.S. Steel, stated, "Hard work is the best investment a man can make." In a speech in New York on September 7, 1902, Theodore Roosevelt said, "Far and away the best prize that life offers is the chance to work hard at work worth doing." Horace said, "Life grants nothing . . . without hard work." Solomon wrote, "Those who work hard will prosper" (Proverbs 13:4).

At the end of a day of hard work, whether at the office or outside in my yard, I feel good. Sure, I might be tired or my muscles might ache, but I have a feeling of accomplishment. Hard work can also keep me out of trouble. As Voltaire wrote in *Candide*, "Work saves us from three great evils: boredom, vice and need." When thinking about why work is so important, there are four challenges we would be wise to consider.

AVOID EXTREMES

Life requires balance in many areas. The old saying about moderation in all things has a lot of merit. Extremes might be exciting, but they are also dangerous. In terms of work, there is the extreme of too little work (laziness) and too much work (drivenness). The goal is hard work—active but not all-consuming, focused but not obsessive, determined but not inflexibly stubborn.

Laziness takes us nowhere. It blocks growth. Unmotivated or halfhearted effort is really no effort at all. Emerson wrote, "Without work one finishes nothing." Laziness traps us in immaturity. A lazy person is rarely successful, respected, or happy. It's interesting how many times Solomon warned about the dangers of laziness. He said, "A lazy fellow has trouble all through life" (Proverbs 15:19, TLB). The opposite side of laziness is drivenness, where work becomes your life. When you are driven, it's easy to become obsessed with goals rather than people. Your focus is primarily on accomplishments. It's easy to lose your sense of true priorities, and stress blocks you from being able to relax, laugh, or have fun.

Laziness gets you nothing, but drivenness rarely gets you what you really want. If you work hard, you give 100 percent when you need to but stop at a reasonable point. I work hard each day helping people with their struggles, and while driving home I do my best to move my thoughts away from work. By the time I arrive home, I want my focus to be on my family.

PRACTICE EXECUTION

Execution is the discipline of getting things done. It involves following a dream through to reality. Anything that is really worthwhile requires discipline, and discipline is hard work. M. Scott Peck, in The Road Less Traveled, insists that "without discipline we can solve nothing." Discipline gives our hard work direction.

Execution is like a car, and discipline is the fuel that keeps things moving. Larry Burkett stated that "those who are successful in any field . . . have a desire to achieve that is coupled with discipline." To execute your goals, you must demonstrate discipline in each of the following six areas.

① **Plan:** Know where you want to end up. Set clear, specific, realistic goals. Take the time to think through a problem, do your research, and consult with others. Without a plan, you won't reach your goal.

② **Prepare:** The Boy Scout motto is "Be prepared." Good preparation can save you time and energy and can protect you from failure.

③ **Push:** This is where you roll up your sleeves and do the necessary tasks. It may be challenging, overwhelming, and exhausting. That's what hard work is all about.

④ **Pace:** Timing can be everything. You must know when to start and when to step back, when to be aggressive and when to be patient. Going too fast can burn you out, while going too slowly can cause you to miss out.

⑤ **Persist:** It is easy to give up when things get too difficult, aren't going as you thought they would, or don't seem fair. To persist is to keep moving forward and to complete what you started.

⑥ **Payoff:** We all like a reward or payoff. It might involve encouragement from others or a sense that we did the right thing. Doing something special to celebrate the completion of hard work can be a wonderful way to wrap up what you just accomplished.

PURSUE EXCELLENCE

We live in a world of mediocrity. Too often we don't take the time or make the effort to do things well. We frequently fall into the trap of thinking that just getting it done is good enough. We have grown used to halfhearted effort. Pearl Buck wrote, "The secret joy in work is contained in one word—excellence. To know how to do something well is to enjoy it." I am not speaking of perfection, which is something none of us will ever achieve. But with excellence we do our very best, given our particular circumstances, whether the job is large or small.

Aiming at excellence is incredibly rewarding, even if we don't hit it. Shake free of mediocrity, and don't accept less than you're capable of. Slow down and do fewer things, but do those things well. Mahatma Gandhi said, "It is the quality of our work which will please God and not the quantity." Martin Luther King Jr. put it this way: "If it falls your lot to be a street sweeper, go on out and sweep streets like Michelangelo painted pictures; sweep streets like Handel and Beethoven composed music; sweep streets like Shakespeare wrote poetry; sweep streets so well that all the host of heaven and earth will have to pause and say, 'Here lived a great street sweeper who did his job well.'"

DO YOUR BEST

The admiral never smiled.

He stared without blinking straight into the eyes of the twenty-two-year-old officer. The young man was saturated with cold sweat, but the admiral kept up the interrogation. Question after question for three long hours.

Finally Admiral Rickover, the father of the nuclear navy, asked something the young man felt good about. "How did you stand in your class at the Naval Academy?"

"Sir, I stood fifty-ninth in a class of 820."

Instead of offering congratulations, the admiral asked, "Did you do your best?"

Jimmy started to say, "Yes sir," but after a quick reflection he gulped and said, "No sir, I didn't always do my best."

"He looked at me for a long while," Jimmy Carter wrote in his autobiography, *Why Not the Best?* "and then turned his chair around to end the interview. He asked one final question, which I have never been able to forget—or to answer. He said, 'Why not?' I sat there for a while, shaken, and then slowly left the room."

Why didn't I work harder or aim higher? Why didn't I finish stronger? These are questions we all must ask ourselves, and each of our answers will be different. But ultimately the most convicting question is the one Jimmy Carter still asks himself: *Why didn't I do my best?*

TODAY'S TOOLS

Prayer

Dear God,

Thank you for giving me the ability to work. Show me what work you would have me do each day—mentally, emotionally, socially, physically, and spiritually.

Forgive me for the times when I am lazy and don't do what needs to be done. Forgive me for the times when I am too driven—times when I have let my determination run over people, principles, and priorities.

Plant discipline in my heart so I will do what needs to be done. Teach me how to plan, prepare, push, pace, and persist. Then when my work is done, give me a positive payoff: a reward, a good feeling, a kind compliment. But if payoff doesn't happen in this life, remind me that you will give me an eternal payoff in the life to come.

Help me to always do my best. Show me the difference between perfec-

tionism and excellence. Stand beside me when I grow tired or discouraged. Strengthen me when I want to give up. Guide me so that all I do is done for you, in a way that brings you honor.

Amen.

Passage

We work hard with our hands.
1 Corinthians 4:12 (NIV)

Practice

① List three examples of laziness and three examples of drivenness in your life. Talk to your spouse or a friend about whether either extreme is a pattern in your life and what you might do to resolve it.

② Of the six Ps described on pages 81–82, which do you struggle with most? Focus on that particular area during the next month and strategize how you might improve your discipline.

③ Make a commitment to do the best you possibly can in all that you do tomorrow. At the end of the day, ask yourself these questions:

In what way was this day different from others?

How did it feel to do my best?

How did people respond to me?

How would it benefit me to repeat this exercise?

RULE ⑩
REST

JON WAS BURNED OUT.

He worked six days a week plus half a day on Sunday. He stayed up late writing reports and frequently fell asleep before he made it to his bed. His alarm clock woke him early, and he started his day so exhausted it took two cups of black coffee before he could keep his eyes open. Jon's life was his work. He was constantly on the go and rarely slowed down. He was successful on the job, but the rest of his life suffered. His marriage fell apart, and his health faltered. He didn't have time for fun, and he didn't know how to relax.

At the age of forty-five, Jon had a breakdown. It started with panic attacks and ended with an inability to concentrate on anything for more than three minutes.

"What can I do?" Jon asked his doctor. "I feel like I'm going crazy."

His doctor looked him square in the eye. "My prescription is simple—rest."

Hard work is important, but it must be balanced with rest. Without rest we grow tired and lose our focus. Our minds become dull, our hearts anxious, our bodies listless, our relationships frustrating, and our spirits empty. Life wears us down and depletes our energy. Rest fills us up and reenergizes us. Rest is like an oasis in the midst of a hot and hectic desert. It is cool, calm, and completely refreshing. There is nothing else quite like it. So in this desert called life, which can so easily sap all our strength, here are three types of oases that nurture a fulfilled life.

A GOOD NIGHT'S SLEEP

Sleep is one of the most important things we do. It renews, restores, and rejuvenates us. Ours is a tired generation, filled with fatigue and exhaustion. We are worn out at every level—mentally, emotionally, physically, socially, and spiritually. As I've spoken to thousands of worn-out people, I'm surprised at how frequently the problem is not getting a good night's sleep. If you ignore this area of your life, you will collapse at each of the five levels—mind, body, spirit, heart, and relationships.

You need a good quality and quantity of sleep. You can't cheat either without paying a high price. There is nothing more wonderful than waking from a restful sleep with the energy and excitement to take on a new, glorious day.

Here are some suggestions for when you lay your head on the pillow tonight:

① Sleep six to eight hours.
② Don't go to bed angry.
③ Unwind and relax in the hour before sleep.
④ Play calming music.
⑤ Imagine something positive as you fade off.
⑥ Pray as you prepare for sleep.

After a solid night of restful sleep, you awake thinking more clearly, with life looking brighter. You also find it easier to reach out to others and be motivated to draw close to God. Without sleep you are unable to pay attention. James Maas, a specialist in sleep research at Cornell University, said, "Good sleep is the best predictor of life span and quality of life."

A RELAXING DAY OFF

Moses told the people of Israel, "In six days the LORD made heaven and earth, but on the seventh day he stopped working and was refreshed" (Exodus 31:17). We all need to set aside a weekly day of rest. This can be a special day when we don't work or even talk about work. In a busy, frantic, do-as-much-as-you-can world, we desperately need a day set apart to slow down and catch our breath. We are a "doing" people who need a time of simply "being." We are surrounded by constant stimulation, activities, temptations, and opportunities. One day out of seven, we need to stop and say no. So take off your shoes, relax, and stay a while.

Isaiah wrote that God "will make rivers in the dry wasteland so my chosen people can be refreshed" (Isaiah 43:20). In the Hebrew language the word for *refresh* means "to breathe." As people race so rapidly from place to place, I've noticed that many don't really breathe. They huff and puff and take quick, short breaths, but they don't fill their lungs and breathe deeply. To be refreshed you must be intentional. You must choose to take the day off. If you don't, your day of rest will quickly get filled up and look like every other hectic day of the week. A day of rest heals our bodies and spirits. It renews us.

A set-aside day need not be static or boring. It is a gift to yourself that adds depth to your life and allows you to be more effective in the other six days of your week. Here are a few ideas for activities to do on your relaxing day off:

- read and study

- play with friends or family

- walk or hike

- visit and talk with others

- attend church

- pray

- write letters or journal

- enjoy the beauty of music or nature

BREAKS AND GETAWAYS

We all need to find times and places to retreat from the onslaught of people, noise, and activity that bombards us every day. Even Jesus needed to escape the crowds. He would get up early in the cool of the morning to be alone with God. At other times he would ask the disciples to take him to the far side of the lake in their fishing boat. We all need breaks and getaways. These moments might be as simple as five quiet minutes in the early morning or an afternoon walk in a park, or as elaborate as a weekend escape at a retreat center.

These escapes become a sanctuary of tranquility within an overwhelming whirlwind. In this sanctuary of solitude, silence, and stillness, amazing things happen that rarely happen elsewhere. *Solitude* conveys the absence of distraction, *silence* is the absence of noise, and *stillness* refers to the absence of activity.

SOLITUDE

Solitude deepens us. Henri Nouwen called it "the furnace of transformation," for what happens in solitude always affects what happens outside it. Oswald Chambers wrote, "Solitude with God repairs the damage done by the fret and noise and clamor of the world." For me, solitude is a beautiful place where I can close out the negativity and pressures that try to steal my peace. This place is my backyard with sunlight filtering through the firs or a sunset at the ocean or an early morning drive to my office. Chuck Swindoll wrote, "Solitude is the cultivation of serenity, a deliberate moving toward peacefulness and contentment, which breeds a sense of security within." Solitude is good company, and it is as close as the next moment or your own backyard.

SILENCE

Noise distracts, annoys, interrupts, entertains, and wounds us. Jochen Schacht stated, "Our ears are not made for a noisy world." Modern life is so loud. We are surrounded by radios, televisions, telephones, computers, CD players, cell phones, and a thousand other invasive sounds. In fact, we are frequently uncomfortable with silence. We avoid it, fight it, fill it. Yet Mother Teresa said that "God . . . cannot be found in noise and restlessness. God is the friend of silence. See how nature—trees, flowers, grass—grows in silence. See the stars, the moon and the sun, how they move in silence."

Silence is good. It is where we find ourselves and God. It is a place where stress fades and peace grows. In *Meditations on Silence*, Sister Wendy Beckett wrote, "Entering into silence is like stepping into cool clear water. The dust and debris are quietly washed away, and we are purified of our triviality. This cleansing takes place whether we are conscious of it or not: The very choice of silence . . . washes away the day's grime." I don't know about you, but there are certainly days when I need the grime washed away.

STILLNESS

Stillness is an essential part of growing deeper. Pam Vredevelt wrote that "perhaps stillness is a prerequisite for knowing." Stillness is not something we do; it's something we don't do. It sounds easy, but it's not. It takes practice and discipline to develop stillness of mind, heart, and body. I'm like most people—I hate waiting. I'm impatient. I want something to happen, and I want it to happen now. So when I read David's words, "Wait patiently for the LORD" (Psalm 27:14), I cringe a little. But I know he's right, so I wait and I practice being still. It's a difficult lesson, but movement without wisdom and direction is either wasted or dangerous. Therefore, I wish to follow the counsel of François Fénelon, a seventeenth-century spiritual adviser: "Learn to wait for God. Do not move until he directs you."

Stillness draws you closer to yourself and God. The psalmist gives us God's perspective: "Be still, and know that I am God" (Psalm 46:10, NIV). When we embrace solitude while being silent and still, we will receive an amazing awareness of God's presence. As John Baillie wrote in *A Diary of Private Prayer*, "All day long have I toiled and striven; but now, in stillness of heart and in the clear light of thine eternity, I would ponder the pattern my life has been weaving." Stillness opens our eyes and ears to our master's movements. So as T. S. Eliot prayed, "Teach us to sit still."

In the middle of her life, Anne Morrow Lindbergh left her hectic schedule for a few weeks on the North Atlantic coast. She stayed alone in a secluded beach cottage with no heat, no telephone, no water, no rug, no curtains. She went away to rest and relax and reflect. In the process of getting away, Anne discovered the wonder of life, and she journaled her contemplations in the best-selling *Gift from the Sea*. Here she wrote, "It is a difficult lesson to learn today—to . . . deliberately practice the art of solitude for an hour or a day or a week." As she adjusted to her time of rest, she concluded that "every person . . . should be alone sometime during the year, some part of each week, and each day." Anne Morrow Lindbergh learned about rest, and in so doing she discovered that life is more than activity and hectic schedules. Without solitude, silence, and stillness, Anne's getaway would have been just another two-week period on a busy calendar. But instead, it fostered reflections that gave her new meaning.

The steps of solitude, silence, and stillness are key in our search for abundant life. They help us to see vividly, hear clearly, and feel fully God's presence. As you practice these steps, carefully consider where you are headed and what sort of life you would like to be living. Let rest rejuvenate you and give you renewed purpose. Don't put it off. Let today be the beginning of your capturing a moment or two of true rest—whether it be in solitude, silence, or stillness.

TODAY'S TOOLS

Prayer

Dear God,

Thank you that you have invited me to rest in you. You are my Rock and my protection. I need not be afraid or worried as long as I trust in you.

Let me sleep deeply and peacefully so I may awake rejuvenated and reenergized. Give me sweet dreams to share with all I meet.

Remind me of how you took a day of rest and commanded us to do likewise. Forgive me for letting your day be contaminated with obligations, activities, and distractions that take me away from focusing on you.

Encourage me to take breaks and getaways so I might gently ease into your precious rest. Help me find a place of solitude so you might refresh my soul. Keep me silent so I might hear your voice. Teach me to sit still so you might renew my strength. As I learn to rest—mentally, emotionally, physically, relationally, spiritually—guide me to a deeper relationship with you. Protect me from being worn out and burned out by this crazy, mixed-up world.

Let your rest bring me your joy.

Amen.

Passage

I will give you rest—everything will be fine for you.
Exodus 33:14

Practice

① Of the suggestions on page 88, which ones do you need to use to help you get more restful sleep?

② List three things you might do or not do to truly give you a day of rest.

③ Find a space of solitude—someplace you can get away from people—and go there alone for an hour.

④ Set aside at least ten minutes a day for one week when you can practice silence and stillness. After each time, write what you thought about and how you felt during those ten minutes.

RULE ⓫
CLING TO THE POSITIVES

HE WAS NUMBER 119,104.

Viktor Frankl was a psychiatrist. He was also an inmate for three years at Auschwitz and other Nazi concentration camps during World War II. In his book *Man's Search for Meaning*, Dr. Frankl wrote about being cold, hungry, naked, and frightened. He was beaten, humiliated, and pushed to the brink of human suffering.

How could a person survive such cruel and horrific conditions? Dr. Frankl wrote that the Gestapo could take everything away from people except their attitudes. They could choose to cling to the positives. If they did that, there was hope. If they didn't, they were doomed. If people focused on the suffering and gave up, they would soon die. Frankl wrote, "Woe to him who saw no more sense in his life, no aim, no purpose, and therefore no point in carrying on. He was soon lost."

Dr. Frankl discovered this amazing truth: If we cling to the positives, we can thrive in the worst of all situations. Yet we are surrounded by negativity—it pushes and pressures us each day of our lives. And if we let it into our minds or hearts, it will spread like a wildfire until negative thoughts and feelings consume us. Soon we begin scattering sparks of negativity to everyone we meet.

To have a great day we must cling to the positives. Doing so allows us to see clearly, to have the right perspective, and to meet our goals. We can be optimistic because we know God cares about us and is ultimately in control. We need to be realistic about our brokenness, but we can be optimistic because we know that God is willing to heal and forgive. Here are five basic ideas that will move us in that direction.

FLEE NEGATIVITY

Negativity kills. It kills joy and relationships and ideas. It kills enthusiasm and motivation. Ultimately it kills hope. If you expect negativity, it will happen. If you ponder negativity, you will become discouraged. If you dwell in negativity, you will become trapped. If you share negativity, you will drive people away.

I despise negativity because I see how much it hurts and destroys people. As a psychologist, I frequently work with good, kindhearted people who have allowed negativity to take hold of their lives. Three of the most common ways negativity takes hold are comparison, perfectionism, and downhill thinking.

Comparison. I wish I could write as well as Max Lucado, be as compassionate as Mother Teresa, and play basketball like Michael Jordan. The more I consider what I don't have or can't do, the less I am able to see what God has given me. In 1927 an obscure lawyer from Indiana, Max Ehrmann, wrote a code for healthy living called "Desiderata." In it he said, "If you compare yourself with others, you may become vain or bitter, for always there will be greater and lesser persons than yourself." When we compare, we focus on our own shortcomings rather than our strengths—and thus breed negativity. Remember, you have unique talents and abilities. Get your eyes off others, and look at what God wants to do with you.

Perfectionism. No one is perfect. We all make mistakes, and we all fail at times. If you aim at the unattainable, you will end up frustrated and defeated. Accept your weaknesses and failures, but at the same time try to do your best. Aim at excellence, not perfection. Mistakes happen and failures occur. Forgive yourself and learn from what has happened. If others can't accept your imperfections, they are not being realistic or compassionate. Perfectionism comes from unrealistic expectations about life, others, or yourself. If you aren't perfect, you are human.

Downhill thinking. Negative thinking will make you negative. As you think, so you will be. Marcus Aurelius believed that "a man's life is what his thoughts make of it." So take charge of your thoughts. To focus on the negative will send your life on a downhill slide.

- Don't look for the negative.

- Don't expect the negative.

- Don't exaggerate the negative.

- Don't dwell on the negative.

Ralph Waldo Emerson summed it up by saying, "A man is what he thinks about all day long."

LOOK FOR POSITIVES IN EVERY SITUATION

Our focus will affect our attitudes. If we look for the best, we will find it. So I try to do what the apostle Paul suggested. He said we should fix our thoughts on "what is true, and honorable, and right, and pure, and lovely, and admirable. Think about things that are excellent and worthy of praise" (Philippians 4:8).

These eight things provide a positive focus. They help build attitudes that can rise above all the negative influences of this world. To focus on the negative gives it power, but to focus on the positive gives *you* power. Martha Washington wrote, "I've learned from experience that the greater part of our happiness or misery depends on our dispositions and not on our circumstances."

You can miss the best things in life if you have the wrong attitude. In *Dream a New Dream*, Dale Galloway wrote that your attitude can "make you or break you." Holding on to a positive attitude can make all the difference in the world. You are in charge of your attitude. Steer in the right direction, and you might be surprised at what comes about. As Dr. Robert Schuller said, "When it's dark, look for the stars."

I want to be an optimist—one who sees the best and believes the best. Winston Churchill declared that "an optimist sees the opportunity in every difficulty." Optimists do not give up. They are excited and challenged by the amazing possibilities that rest in almost every situation. A healthy optimist is neither naive, unrealistic, or blind. They simply see beyond the limits and challenges that absorb the focus of most people. Optimism is a choice that sheds positive light wherever we go. Positive attitudes tend to make our optimism come true. And the longer and stronger we hold on to it, the better we feel and the brighter the world around us appears. Helen Keller, though blind and deaf, was a delightful optimist. She wrote, "No pessimist ever discovered the secret of the stars or sailed to an uncharted land or opened a new doorway for the human spirit."

FILL YOUR LIFE WITH POSITIVES

I love positive people. They energize and excite me. Negative people wear me out. Complainers and discouragers frustrate me and, over time, sap my energy. In fact, negative people can make me negative. So when I'm feeling down, I want to stand close to an optimist and soak in his or her sunshine. Just as I am drawn to positive people, so are others. Therefore, I want to be someone who energizes and encourages others. I want to be an optimist who can help pull others out of the mud and grime of this world.

When I feel stressed or overwhelmed, I yearn for a positive setting—a park, a beach, a forest, a garden. These are positive places for me, where the beauty and peacefulness of nature can calm my spirit. A positive atmosphere can refresh me in amazing ways. The sound of water, a warm breeze, a peaceful landscape, and a multicolored sunset are just a few of the positive settings that bring me joy.

Positive things allow me to wash all the negatives out of my mind. Yet the most effective means of filling our lives with positives is to think beyond this world. The apostle Paul wrote, "Think about the things of heaven" (Colossians 3:2). For no matter how dark or ugly or negative this world may get, God can give us hope. Knowing that he loves us, forgives us, and has a great dream for us can have an incredibly positive effect on our lives. Thomas Moore wrote that "earth has no sorrow that Heaven cannot heal."

REPLACE EVERY NEGATIVE WITH A POSITIVE

No matter how hard we try, sooner or later negativity will try to pull us down. But we can fight it and change our attitudes. In his international best seller *The Power of Positive Thinking*, Norman Vincent Peale wrote, "Whenever a negative thought . . . comes to mind, deliberately voice a positive thought to cancel it out." We all have negative, unhealthy, and hurtful thoughts every single day. When they come, we can either invite them to stay or kick them out. But if we kick them out and don't replace them, the negative will return. Dr. Peale used three positive affirmations to keep the negatives from returning. He said to himself, *God is with me; God is helping me; God is guiding me.* Many people use positive affirmations to keep the door to their minds secure from unwelcome intruders.

Yet too often we are our own worst enemies. We tell ourselves we can't do it or we have failed or we are stupid. We give up or get angry. Our negative self-talk can be our defeat. So we must choose to replace it with positive self-talk. I believe the best positive affirmations come directly from the Bible. Here are five affirmations I suggest you use often so they become a natural part of your self-talk:

① This is the day the LORD has made. We will rejoice and be glad in it. (Psalm 118:24)

② With God all things are possible. (Matthew 19:26, NIV)

③ If God is for us, who can ever be against us? (Romans 8:31)

④ Be sure of this: I am with you always. (Matthew 28:20)

⑤ The LORD your God . . . will neither fail you nor abandon you. (Deuteronomy 31:6)

These positive affirmations can become the basis of positive thinking. So use them throughout the day whenever a negative thought pops up. As Mike Huckabee, the governor of Arkansas, reminds us, "Positive thinking is powerful medicine." It can heal the worst negative.

BE THANKFUL

Being thankful keeps us focused on the positive. While dwelling on what we are thankful for, it is difficult to be negative. Charlie "Tremendous" Jones claimed that "learning to be thankful covers it all." Every day I try to review at least a few of the things I'm thankful for. Today at different times, I've thanked God for my three kids, sunshine, a tall glass of water, friends, health, and my wife.

Thankfulness leads to optimism, which overflows into hope and joy. Gratitude reminds us of all we have. It causes us to embrace life with a sense of excitement and expectation. It brings us to a point of appreciation and celebration.

Ingratitude is a denial of reality and the goodness of God. It is greedy (wanting more) and blind (unable to see all that it has). As we cling to the positives, we will become more and more thankful. Erwin McManus wrote in Uprising, "When we are grateful, we are most fully alive. Gratitude allows us to absorb every possible pleasure from a moment. When your heart is full of gratitude, life paints itself in far brighter and more vivid colors."

If we stop and think about it, we all have a lot to be thankful for. M. R. Vincent wrote that "the Christian is suspended between blessings received and blessings hoped for, so he should always give thanks." The world is full of blessings. Even failures, difficulties, and disappointments can actually be blessings. We often feel thankful only if things go our way. But I believe we can and should be thankful regardless of what happens.

The difficulty in being thankful is really a crisis of creativity. We take so much for granted that our eyes grow old. We don't recognize the incredible things that surround us each day. If we would only stop and look around, we would see a multitude of things for which to be thankful. An ancient prayer speaks of this: "For all thy blessings known and unknown, remembered and forgotten, we give thee thanks." Anne Lamott's book *Traveling Mercies* recounts the joys and sorrows of her life. Her journey has not been an easy one, and yet she ends her book with a bold statement of "Thank you. Thank you. Thank you." Maybe that's the way we should end every day, every conversation, every task.

By the time Bill Van Atta was thirteen, he was legally blind. His father beat him when he ran into doors or misplaced tools, telling him that all he was good for was selling pencils on a street corner. Then life got harder. He had two bouts of what was diagnosed as terminal cancer and multiple surgeries to remove twelve tumors on his spine, which left him in chronic pain. Yet all who know him shake their heads in amazement, saying it's almost impossible to find a man more content than Bill Van Atta.

Bill chose to cling to positives. He worked his way through school, passed the bar exam, and is now a lawyer in Ontario, Oregon. He regularly speaks to the county historical society, has been president of the county bar association, has made five country and gospel CDs, and has won numerous awards. Everywhere he goes people encourage him, and in turn he encourages everyone he meets.

"I'm a blessed man," Bill says. "My blindness taught me about new ways of seeing. . . . I've learned patience and that strength comes from struggle. I learned I could languish or I could live. . . . Life is about the choices you make hourly. You can be bitter and turn inward or turn outward. I choose to embrace life."

Bill Van Atta discovered what Viktor Frankl discovered, along with almost every other successful person: You've got to cling to positives. And you've got to start today.

TODAY'S TOOLS

Prayer

Dear God,

Forgive me for how I have allowed the world to squeeze me into its negativity. Protect me from being sucked into all the negative influences that can shape my thoughts and emotions.

Open my eyes to the many positives that surround me every day. Help me to focus on all that is good and beautiful so I don't take these gifts for granted.

Bring positive people into my life and show me how to treat them with love. Then teach me to be a more protective person to others by encouraging them with my words and ways.

When negative thoughts slip into my mind, show me how to replace them with something positive. Remind me that your presence is the most powerful thing in my life. When I struggle, let me know that you are close by my side, protecting me and guiding me.

Thank you for your many blessings. Thank you for the good and positive gifts you have given me through the years. But most of all, thank you for your amazing love.

Amen.

Passage

I have learned the secret of being content in any and every situation.
Philippians 4:12 (NIV)

Practice

① Make a list of three types of negativity you need to flee.
② Think about one positive person and one positive place. Reflect on how each one lifts your spirits and protects you from negativity.
③ Consider five positive affirmations that encourage you (you may consider the affirmations on page 102). Write down these affirmations on a piece of paper and carry it with you in your wallet or purse. Whenever you fall into negative self-talk, pull out this paper and read through each positive affirmation.
④ Take a good friend to lunch and share three things that you are truly thankful for.

RULE ⑫
DRAW CLOSE TO GOD

THE BOY WAS BARELY ALIVE.

Dr. Winters was called at 1:00 a.m. and told to rush to the hospital. His hands were the only ones in the city skilled enough to save the boy. Since every minute was crucial, he took a shortcut through one of the most dangerous neighborhoods of the city. At a stoplight a man in a dirty flannel shirt forced open the door, pulled him out of his seat, and ordered, "Give me your car!"

The doctor explained that he was on the way to the hospital for emergency surgery, but the thief wouldn't listen. He took the car and sped off. Dr. Winters ran through the streets trying to make it to the hospital on foot. An hour later he finally made it.

"You're too late," the head nurse said. "The boy died about thirty minutes ago. His father is in the chapel. He can't understand why you never came."

Dr. Winters walked to the chapel and there, weeping at the altar, was a man in a dirty flannel shirt. The boy's father looked up at the doctor and in horror realized what he had just done. He had pushed away the only one in the city who could have saved his son.

How often do we do this to God? We push him away for many reasons.

Maybe we don't have time for him, we have blamed him for some misfortune, or we just don't think about him. Pushing God away, however we do it, is self-defeating. For the core of faith is drawing close to God. The closer we get, the clearer we see and the calmer we feel. Faith gives us confidence and strength and courage.

A day without God is severely limited. In fact, life doesn't even make sense without God. He gives us a purpose, and without a purpose we are like a ship lost on the ocean with neither a map nor a rudder. As actress Kathy Ireland says, "My faith is important. I have nothing without it." As I help people deal with the hurts and difficulties of life, I see even those who have no experience with God reaching up to him. When we are alone or heartbroken or overwhelmed, we yearn for closeness and comfort from the maker of all.

James gives us the simple solution to this deep yearning: "Come close to God, and God will come close to you" (James 4:8). There are many ways to draw close and connect with God. Here are five important ones.

SEEK GOD

God is not hiding. David told his son Solomon, "If you seek him, you will find him" (1 Chronicles 28:9). God is right next to each of us. He guides our way and guards our backs. He is above us and below us. He is everywhere at every moment. God is in a beautiful sunset and the smile of a stranger. God is so big and yet so personal. Unfortunately we frequently don't see because we don't look.

Every day I wish to seek God. Wherever I am and whatever I am doing, I want to find a glimpse of him. Because that glimpse, no matter how big or small, is what gives me everything I need to be whole and healthy. As David wrote when he was in the wilderness of Judah, "O God . . . I earnestly search for you. My soul thirsts for you; my whole body longs for you in this parched and weary land" (Psalm 63:1). Augustine, in his *Confessions*, wrote, "Thou has formed us for thyself, and our hearts are restless till they find rest in thee." So much of what we seek—success, possessions, status, acceptance, respect—is ultimately empty and unfulfilling without God.

As we seek God, he seeks us. He pursues us more persistently than we pursue him. Yet God is a gentleman; he will not force himself upon us or push himself into our lives without a proper invitation. In a delightful little book called *The Air I Breathe*, Louie Giglio puts it this way: "God is always seeking you. Every sunset. Every clear blue sky. Each ocean wave. The starry host of night. He blankets each new day with the invitation, 'I am here.'" All we need to do is look and listen, for he is there.

KNOW HIM

To know a little about God is to understand a lot about everything else. As we seek God, the desire to know him more and more deeply will consume us. Yet A. W. Tozer wrote in *The Pursuit of God* that "the world is perishing for lack of the knowledge of God." J. I. Packer takes this thought a bit deeper in *Knowing God* by writing, "Disregard the study of God, and you sentence yourself to stumble and blunder through life blindfolded, as it were, with no sense of direction and no understanding of what surrounds you. This way you can waste your life and lose your soul." We must know God to know ourselves and how to live abundantly in this broken world.

The more we set aside time to know God, the closer we move to him. And the closer we move, the more we come to know. Yet a finite mind can never fully grasp an infinite God. We cannot conceive how great he is or how majestic his nature. Our thoughts cannot capture his power, and our words cannot express his awesomeness. We use words like infinite, holy, perfect, eternal, all-knowing, and all-powerful, but our understanding of these attributes of God is so small. I do not write this to discourage but rather to keep perspective. All who are wise will strive to know God, yet we must keep in mind that this is a humbling and exhilarating task. J. I. Packer challenges us: "What makes life worthwhile is having a big enough objective, something which catches our imagination and lays hold of our allegiance; and this the Christian has in a way that no other person has. For what higher, more exalted, and more compelling goal can there be than to know God?"

LOVE HIM

When Jesus was asked what was the greatest of all commandments, he said that it was to "love the LORD your God with all your heart, all your soul, all your mind, and all your strength" (Mark 12:30). To know God is to love him with all of who we are. When we realize that in the midst of his infinite power there is gentleness and mercy, our hearts soften. God's love for us causes us to love him. What other response could one have to such an amazing love?

Out of our love comes a desire to express our delight. J. Oswald Sanders wrote, "Worship flows from love. . . . Where love is deep, worship will overflow." Love without expression becomes suspect. If love is kept quiet, it fades and may even die. Worship is an integral part of our faith. Amy Carmichael reminds us that without worship "we so often run dry. We do not give time enough to what makes for depth, and so we are shallow; a wind, quite a little wind, can ruffle our surface; a little hot sun, and all the moisture in us evaporates. It should not be so." Love expressed is both refreshing and delightful.

To worship God is to acknowledge him. It is to recognize his greatness and majesty and mercy in the world around us. It is to thank him for who he is and what he has done and what he will do. It is to tell others about the magnificent God of the universe.

TRUST HIM

Trust in people, and they'll let you down. Trust in things, and they'll fall apart. Trust in yourself, and you are doomed to disappointment. So what or whom can you rely on? God alone is worthy of trust. Solomon gave the instruction to "trust in the LORD with all your heart; do not depend on your own understanding" (Proverbs 3:5). The more we get to know God, the more trustworthy we find him to be. Linda Dillow wrote, "Trusting God is a moment-by-moment challenge possible only when we focus on his character." We can trust him totally because

- he is good

- he is in control

- he is wise

- he loves us

- he is with us

David recorded this promise from God: "I will guide you along the best pathway for your life. I will advise you and watch over you" (Psalm 32:8).

To trust God is one of the smartest things you can do. Throughout the psalms God is seen as a rock, a refuge, a hiding place, a fortress, a protector, and a shelter in times of storm. He is trustworthy when it's dark, when anxieties overwhelm us, when dreams fall apart, and when nothing is going our way. God is also trustworthy during the day, when all is smooth or when distractions pull us away. John Calvin reassured us that "trusting God allows for gratitude in prosperity, patience in adversity, and a wonderful security." As we trust God we lean on him, or as Amy Carmichael, a missionary to India, suggested: We can tuck ourselves into him. So do what François Fénelon, a seventeenth-century French archbishop, suggested: "Pray for strength and faith enough to trust yourself completely to God. . . . Give yourself as completely as you can to God. Do so until your final breath, and he will never desert you."

FOLLOW HIM

If you truly trust God, why not follow him? As Elijah spoke to the people at Mount Carmel, he put it simply: "If the LORD is God, follow him!" (1 Kings 18:21). Jesus said, "Take up your cross, and follow me" (Matthew 16:24). Following God means to *obey* him, *honor* him, and *imitate* him. Anyone serious about drawing closer to God will see that each of these is a symbol of how important God is to you.

Obey. Jesus said, "If you love me, obey my commandments" (John 14:15), and one of his greatest commandments is to "love your neighbor as yourself" (Matthew 22:39). Therefore, I want to treat others respectfully and with kindness. I try to treat others as Jesus would treat them: with patience, understanding, encouragement, and love.

Obedience can also mean stepping out of our comfort zones and taking a risk to follow him. Abraham is a great example of obedience; James wrote that he was trusting God so much that he was willing to do whatever God told him to do (James 2:22). Remember these wise words by Michael Molinos: "Obedience is ready at any time, with no excuse and no delay."

Honor. Solomon told us to "honor the LORD with your wealth" (Proverbs 3:9). Part of loving and following God is giving regularly to him. As we give him our time, talents, and treasures, we draw closer to him. However, honor is more than giving. Respecting God, speaking of him reverently, being aware of him, and teaching our children about his importance are all powerful ways of showing honor.

Imitate. As we follow God, we try to be like him. The psalmist wrote, "Walk only in his paths" (Psalm 119:3). Benjamin Franklin said to "imitate Jesus." The term Christian refers to one being like Christ. He is our example.

To have a great day, we must follow God. He is our maker, who knows us better than we know ourselves. So follow his example and listen to his words. Jesus said, "My sheep listen to my voice; I know them, and they follow me" (John 10:27). So as we struggle through each day, in whatever our circumstances, we must draw close to God. We need to follow him and let him be our guide.

Drawing close to God allows us to draw close to all that is good. It enriches our every experience and brings meaning to everything—regardless of how adverse or obscure. As we intentionally *seek* him, we come to know him through a few precious and powerful glimpses of what is ultimately beyond our limited comprehension. The more we get to know him, the more we come to love and trust him. Then the only rational response is to follow him. Altogether these five verbs draw us closer to God and deepen our connection with the infinite. We become attuned to his eternal voice with its wisdom and guidance and comfort. This alone makes life worthwhile.

Once Billy Graham was asked, "Of all the presidents and people you've met, of all the crusades and conferences you've held, of all the honors you've received, what was the highlight of your long and successful life?"

Without hesitation, his response was that it was his time alone each day when he could truly draw closer to God. Everything else paled when compared to spending time connecting with the Lord and maker of the universe.

TODAY'S TOOLS

Prayer

Dear God,

I yearn for you. Keep me seeking after you every moment of every day. Show me your face everywhere I go, and let me feel your presence.

Thank you for wanting me to know you and for making yourself knowable. Forgive me for not trying to know you more. Open my eyes to your Word and your creation so that I might get a clearer glimpse of you.

You are so gentle and loving that I sometimes forget how mighty and holy you are. Allow me to humble myself before your infinite power, remembering that your infinite greatness deserves my ultimate respect.

Thank you for being so dependable and trustworthy. You are my rock, my refuge, my hiding place, my fortress, my protector, and my shelter in times of storm. For this I am eternally grateful.

I love you and praise you for all you are. I praise you for your wisdom and the way you guide me when I stop to listen. I praise you for your love, which is more amazing than I can even begin to understand.

Help me to follow you wherever you may lead me. Strengthen me as I learn to better obey, honor, and imitate you. As I work on drawing closer to you, thank you for your willingness to draw close to me.

Amen.

Passage

As the deer longs for streams of water, so I long for you, O God. I thirst for God.

Psalm 42:1-2

Practice

① Find a quiet place and consider three things you've done in the past that have helped you draw closer to God. Which of these things could you do this week?

② Meet with a friend and write down as many words as you can think of to describe God. Discuss how these words can have an impact on your life.

③ What have you done in the past week that shows how much you love

God? What are you willing to do during this coming week to show your love?

④ Which of the following are easy for you to do? Which are difficult? Why?

Seek God.

Know God.

Fear God.

Love God.

Praise God.

Trust God.

Obey God.

Honor God.

Imitate God.

Thank God.

RULE ⓭
CULTIVATE COMMUNITY

BILL AND JIM WERE BUDDIES.

They both fought in the trenches during World War I. One day as they charged the enemy, the firefight was severe. The commanding officer called for his men to retreat to their trenches. As they followed their orders, Jim was shot. He fell to the ground, unable to get himself to a place of safety. Bill made it back to the trenches and was shocked to discover that his good friend hadn't.

The shelling continued. The battle grew worse. Bill could see Jim lying unprotected, all alone in the middle of a horrible battlefield. Bill wanted to go out and help him, comfort him, encourage him. The commanding officer refused to let Bill leave the trenches. He said, "It's too dangerous, and besides, Jim is dying. It's too late for him. You're a good soldier, and I won't lose you trying to save someone who has been fatally wounded."

Ignoring his orders, Bill faced the bullets and ran for his friend. With great risk and courage, Bill dragged Jim back to the safety of the trenches, but it was too late. Jim was dead. The officer was furious. "What were you thinking? What a stupid risk! Now don't you see what a worthless chance you took?" Bill responded firmly, "It was definitely worth the risk."

"Are you crazy?" asked the commanding officer.

"No," Bill insisted. "It was worth the risk because Jim's last words were, 'Thank you; I knew you'd come.'"

If you're part of a community, you know someone will come. You will not be alone but will always have a place to belong. We were all designed to connect with others. Connection is life, and isolation is death. It is in community that we experience the greatest growth and joy. M. Scott Peck wrote in his book *The Different Drum* that "we humans hunger for genuine community and will work hard to maintain it precisely because it is the way to live most fully, most vibrantly."

We all yearn for intimate alliances and deep friendships with those willing to share their lives. We hope for companions to journey alongside us as we scale the rugged peaks and trek the empty deserts of life. We long for a band of brothers or sisters to protect our backs and fight beside us. This is what John Eldredge calls "fellowships of the heart," and it's what we passionately crave and desperately dream of. After all, we need a place

- to be loved when we're lonely

- to be protected when we're afraid

- to be comforted when we're hurting

- to be taught when we're confused

- to be encouraged when we're downhearted

- to be given hope when all seems dark

True community can provide all of this. Yet community doesn't just happen; it must be carefully and intentionally cultivated. How do we develop a community? Through sharing, forgiving, and comforting each other.

SHARING OUR HEARTS

Healthy communication is crucial to building positive relationships. Without it there is no hope for cultivating community. It's through our words that we get to know, understand, and encourage each other. We share our hearts with each other and go beyond the trap of sharing only facts, incidents, gossip, or trivia. This sort of small talk has its place, but after a while it is not truly satisfying. It gives the illusion of connection, but it does not provide closeness. I yearn for something more. I want to hear about your worries and fears, your strengths and weaknesses, your passions and dreams. Then I can love and accept the real you, not a fuzzy vapor that disappears when my arms stretch out for a genuine embrace.

It's easy for me to embrace others, but I'm afraid to let you embrace me. I don't know if I can trust you. Too many people have betrayed me in the past, so why should I trust that you won't do the same? When I want to connect, all sorts of emotions get in the way—mistrust, hurt, fear, defensiveness, insecurity, jealousy, guilt, shame, disappointment, frustration. As John Powell wrote in *Why Am I Afraid to Tell You Who I Am?* "If I tell you who I am, you may not like who I am, and it's all I have." Fifty-seven pages later he wrote that "to reveal myself openly and honestly takes the rawest kind of courage."

To cultivate community, I must admit who I am to myself and then confess it to others. I must stop hiding and risk total humiliation. I must step out in faith and expose my dark side, as Brennan Manning does in his book *Ruthless Trust: The Ragamuffin's Path to God*. He cries out, "Is there anyone I can level with? Anyone I dare tell that I am benevolent and malevolent, chaste and randy, compassionate and vindictive, selfless and selfish, that beneath my brave words lives a frightened child, that I dabble in religion and pornography, that I have blackened a friend's character, betrayed a trust, violated a confidence, that I am tolerant and thoughtful, a bigot and a blowhard?"

Communities must be places of safety. This is where we accept each other as we are, with no conditions. This is where we say, "Come as you are. I will stand beside you, and nothing you can do will push me away from you." In his book *Sacred Companions*, David G. Benner said that we all need "a place where anything can be said without fear of criticism or ridicule. . . . It is a place where it is safe to share deepest secrets, darkest fears, most acute sources of shame, most disturbing questions or anxieties. It is a place of grace—a place where others are accepted as they are for the sake of who they may become."

I want a place like this. In a perfect world, community would be the norm rather than the exception. It all must start with sharing our time and our hearts with each other, our families, our friends, our coworkers, our neighbors, and our churches.

FORGIVING EACH OTHER

Life is full of hurts. Every day, in a hundred random and thoughtless ways, people inflict pain on each other. Holding on to this pain distances us from others. To cultivate community and build trust, we must forgive.

It may sound strange, but the first step toward forgiving is to admit how hurt and angry we really are. The fact is, others have been insensitive and cruel. Sometimes it seems easier to pretend the hurt isn't important and try to forget about it. The trouble is, we don't forget. Offenses that wound our hearts accumulate in our memories and keep us from experiencing community. Forgiveness essentially means giving up our right to make other people pay for the wrongs they have committed against us. It's a choice, a decision of the will. Keep in mind that the choice of forgiveness almost always precedes the feeling of forgiveness. That may take time—not because forgiveness doesn't work, but because your emotional wounds still need time to heal.

We must stop rehearsing the pain. Once we have faced what has happened to us, we can be done with reliving the past and rehashing the details. Memories will rise in our minds, but we can choose to put them away and focus on other things. We can then, slowly and cautiously, start the journey toward community.

Forgiveness sets both the offender and the victim free. When we forgive, something inside of us changes. We are set free from the bile and bitterness that eat away at us. When we forgive, we are able to see others more clearly. Forgiveness allows us to step out and grow. If we hold something against someone, we will find it hard to trust that person. We will constantly guard ourselves from the next potential hurt. This is why Martin Luther King Jr. said, "Forgiveness is not an occasional act; it is a permanent attitude."

Forgiveness works both ways. Just as we need to forgive, there are times we need to seek forgiveness. When we become aware that we have hurt someone, even if it was not intentional, we need to do what we can to heal the situation. These five Rs allow anyone who has hurt another to take a giant step toward restoration:

1. **Responsibility:** Accept that your actions or attitudes did harm, regardless of whether the injured person deserved it or had a part in it.
2. **Repentance:** Sincerely and specifically apologize to the person you harmed without blame, excuses, or defensiveness.
3. **Remorse:** Try to see the situation through the injured person's eyes and feel the hurt that he or she feels.
4. **Restitution:** Do something special and meaningful for the person harmed to show that you genuinely regret what you did.
5. **Repair:** Do all you can to return the relationship to the state it was in before the injury.

Lack of forgiveness, either giving it or asking for it, builds walls and blocks community. On the other hand, forgiveness breaks down those walls, allowing compassion, connection, and community to happen.

COMFORTING EACH OTHER

In true community, you feel loved and accepted. You belong. If you are hurting or struggling, others will quickly come alongside you. In community, loneliness is lessened and sometimes even taken away. When a person sees a need, he or she quickly and sacrificially meets it. In a community, people come alongside others without having to be asked.

Community involves binding together with love and loyalty. We commit time, communication, and comfort to each other. Comfort is love in action. It asks, "What are you doing for others?" It makes love real—not sentimental or romantic but sacrificial and hardworking. A community without love ceases to be a community. Dr. Willard Harley wrote in his book *Love Busters* that there are six things that can kill the love in any relationship or community:

① selfish demands
② disrespectful judgments
③ angry outbursts
④ dishonesty
⑤ annoying habits
⑥ independent behavior

Love defers to others, and their needs take precedence over our own. In a community there is an interdependence of love.

Comfort and friendship each grow out of the other. Friendship is like shade on a hot day. A friend knows what we need and doesn't hesitate to provide it. In his book *Our Greatest Gift*, Henri Nouwen wrote about such a friend: "During the most difficult period of my life, when I experienced great anguish and despair, he was there. Many times, he pulled my head to his chest and prayed for me without words but with a spirit-filled silence that dispelled my demons of despair and made me rise up from his embrace with new vitality." This is the sort of friendship and comfort we all yearn for. This is what community is all about.

In 1942, as Nazis occupied Holland, two families fled their homes and went into hiding in what came to be known as the Secret Annex. For two years these families lived isolated from the rest of the world in an old office building. Here in the shadow of discovery and death,

thirteen-year-old Anne Frank wrote about her little community—
how they shared their hearts and encouraged each other. Their time
together was not easy, but they grew close. They learned the importance of acceptance, support, and shared optimism. In so doing, they
made a horrible situation tolerable and even enjoyable at times.

Community can happen anywhere and at any time. If you are willing
to cultivate community, ordinary times will take on a deeper meaning,
and difficult times will not be without hope.

TODAY'S TOOLS

Prayer

Dear God,

*Thank you for community. Thank you for friends and family. Thank you
for all the people you have brought into my life—a community where I can
love and be loved.*

*Give me the courage to honestly share my heart. Help me to listen,
accept, and embrace those who share their hearts with me. Show me a
place of safety and help me to create a place of safety for others.*

*As I draw closer to others, teach me how to forgive freely and how to
sincerely seek the forgiveness of those I have hurt. Soften my heart and
make me a comfort to those around me. I want to encourage and care for
and support others, but sometimes it's so hard. Teach me to comfort others
every chance I can.*

*Challenge me through other people so that I may grow and become a
healthier person. Give me the right words and attitudes so I can strongly,
lovingly challenge others.*

Through the process of community, draw me closer to you. Teach me to build and support community in a way that will truly glorify you.
Amen.

Passage

I want them to be encouraged and knit together by strong ties of love.
Colossians 2:2

Practice

① Consider all the communities you have been involved with during your lifetime. Which of these was the most positive? Why?

② List one person you need to forgive and one person from whom you need to ask forgiveness. Pray over both of these names and ask God what he would have you do. Then do it.

③ When have you most needed comforting? Who reached out, and how did that person show that he or she cared?

RULE ⑭
BE COMMITTED

LIEUTENANT HIROO ONODA was a committed soldier. In 1944 he was stationed alone on the tropical island of Lubang in the Philippines with orders to wage guerrilla warfare against American forces. He did his job well, hiding in the jungle and making solitary raids whenever possible. In 1945 World War II ended, but Lieutenant Onoda would not give up. For twenty-nine years he followed the orders given by his commander, refusing to believe that Japan had lost the war. Living off the land and avoiding search parties, he remained committed to his cause.

Leaflets, newspapers, and letters from friends were dropped into the jungle begging Lieutenant Onoda to surrender. Yet he remained faithful to his mission. It wasn't until March 10, 1974, when he received personal orders from his former commander, that Lieutenant Onoda came out of the jungle, unloaded his bullets, and laid his gun down on the ground. His thirty-year war was finally over.

Now that's commitment!

Another man on another continent wrote the following letter to his girlfriend, explaining why he must break up with her: "There is one thing in which I am in dead earnest about, and that is the Communist cause. It is my life, my business, my religion, my hobby, my sweetheart, my wife, my mistress, my bread and meat. I work at it in the daytime and dream of it at night. Its hold on me grows, not lessens, as time goes on; therefore, I cannot carry on a friendship, a love affair, or even a conversation without relating it to this force which both drives and guides my life. I evaluate people, looks, ideas, and actions according to how they affect the Communist cause, and by their attitude toward it. I've already been in jail because of my ideals, and if necessary, I'm ready to go before a firing squad."

Commitment or lack of commitment defines who we are. Commitments come in many different forms. Lieutenant Onoda was committed to his country, the young man to his ideology. Others may be committed to possessions, politics, hobbies, sports, jobs, health, or the most recent fad. I admire committed people. Their dedication shows that they believe in something, even if I disagree with them or think their belief is trivial.

We all need commitments. To have no commitments is to have no beliefs, no passions, no purposes, and ultimately, no real life. Without them life becomes shallow, mediocre, and meaningless.

Though the quality of our commitment is significant, its object can make it appear either admirable or foolish. Three of the healthiest and most admirable objects of commitment are marriage, family, and God. These commitments are foundational to a wise and abundant life.

COMMIT TO MARRIAGE

A number of years ago I was at a major conference of marriage counselors where the topic was at what point a marriage should be dissolved. The speaker suggested that marriage was a contract and that when the contract was no longer beneficial to either party it should be terminated. Most of those in attendance seemed to agree. I sat in silence until I could handle it no longer. I raised my hand and asked, "What about commitment?"

What happened next shocked me and has disturbed me ever since. The crowd burst into laughter. How sad!

Marriage is sacred. Jesus said, "What God has joined together, let man not separate" (Matthew 19:6, NIV). Marriage is a total, timeless commitment between a husband and a wife; it is also a covenant with God. It must be taken seriously, because God takes it seriously. T. S. Eliot wrote, "Marriage is the greatest test in the world. . . . It is a test of the whole character and affects every action." A good marriage is not easy. It requires overcoming all that can potentially harm your relationship, such as hectic schedules, disappointment, laziness, selfishness, negativity, boredom, debt, misunderstandings, and gradual distancing.

In their book *When Bad Things Happen to Good Marriages*, Drs. Les and Leslie Parrott write, "A good marriage is made up of . . . two people living the love they promise. They are a committed couple." This promise involves a serious commitment to the following five areas:

① **Oneness:** Cling to one another in body, soul, and spirit.
② **Affirmation:** Speak the truth in love, seeking to encourage each other in all you say.
③ **Prioritizing:** Put each other above everything else in your lives except for God.
④ **Protection:** Protect each other physically, financially, emotionally, socially, and spiritually.

⑤ **Endurance:** Take seriously your promise to love and cherish one another for all the days of your life "until death do us part."

Herman H. Kieval sums up all these areas by simply saying that "marriage is a commitment—a decision to do, all through life, that which will express love for one's spouse." In other words, you say to your spouse, "No matter what happens, I will love you."

COMMIT TO FAMILY

Once upon a time there was a town at the foot of a mountain range that got its water from springs high in the hills. The town hired a certain forest dweller to be the Keeper of the Springs. He visited each spring, clearing the springs of fallen leaves, mud, and other debris. Then he made sure the water flowed properly—clean, cold, and pure.

But one day the town council decided it no longer needed a Keeper of the Springs and dismissed him. Soon the water grew brown, slime filled the pipes, and an epidemic spread through the town. Recognizing a mistake had been made, the council quickly rehired the Keeper of the Springs. Within a week the water turned clear, the pipes were cleaned, and the sickness began to fade. From that point on, the town recognized the full value of the Keeper of the Springs.

Each and every parent, grandparent, uncle, and aunt is a Keeper of the Springs for the children in their lives. We need to proactively guard and protect our children from the dangers, foolishness, and evil that so often surround us in this broken world. We need adults who will truly commit themselves to the next generation. Dr. James Dobson wrote in his book

Parenting Isn't for Cowards that "parents can and must train, shape, mold, correct, guide, punish, reward, instruct, warn, teach, and love their kids during the formative years." Children will remember and appreciate the care we show them more than all the stuff we give them.

Being committed to family can be a challenge, but to ignore the challenge is to scar the future. Children need an atmosphere that allows them to grow strong, with branches that reach out and roots that dig deep. As you try to establish this atmosphere for your family, consider practicing the six A's of parenting:

① **Be aware.** Listen to your children, watch them, ask them questions. Discover their likes and dislikes, their dreams and fears, their strengths and weaknesses.

② **Be assertive.** Pass on the lessons you've learned from life. Teach your children the truth. Provide reasonable rules and consistent consequences when those rules are broken.

③ **Be accepting.** Focus on their positives and assist them with their negatives. Don't expect perfection from them, lest they turn and expect it from you. Be patient with them.

④ **Be approachable.** One of the biggest challenges dads face is maintaining too much emotional distance from their children. Spend quality time with them. Laugh with them; play with them; enjoy them.

⑤ **Be affectionate.** Hug your children often, and tell them every day that you love them. Give them compliments, and encourage them instead of criticizing them. Treat them gently and with respect. Treasure them.

⑥ **Be alert.** The world is full of dangers and temptations. Be your
children's protector. Watch over them and warn them. Protect
them without being paranoid.

Most important of all, pray for your children daily.

As Solomon wrote, "Children are a gift from the LORD" (Psalm
127:3). Therefore, commit yourself to them, and pray for them every
day. Remember, they are the future.

COMMIT TO GOD

It was a Sunday morning in 1991. The group of thirty Christians stood
unafraid on the street in Cano, Peru. They wanted the world to see that
they were committed. They prayed and sang to God, in spite of the fact
that some twelve hours before, terrorists had killed their pastor and
burned down their church and many of their houses. Yet they continued
to gather together because nobody could take away their commitment.

Every week millions of Christians gather in other countries under the
threat of death. Each week thousands of Christians are killed simply because they are committed to God. True commitment is being willing to
pay the price. A committed Christian doesn't pray that life will be easy
but rather that he or she will be strong and worthy of Christ's name. As
Saleema, a nineteen-year-old Christian in Pakistan, put it, "I would
rather be hung than betray my Lord." To many people throughout the
world, being committed to God means suffering, persecution, beatings,
imprisonment, loss of friends, destruction of possessions, and even
death. Mother Teresa defined commitment as "Jesus is everything."

So commitment is giving ourselves totally to God. Oswald Chambers wrote, "Shut out every other consideration and keep yourself before God for this one thing only—My Utmost for His Highest. I am determined to be absolutely and entirely for Him and Him alone." This involves fully trusting that God is exactly who he says he is. To be committed to God we must surrender and submit. As Jesus said, "You must turn from your selfish ways, take up your cross, and follow me" (Matthew 16:24). We must follow his call to:

① **Adventure.** The life of faith is full of thrills and excitement. To follow him is to experience life to the fullest, reaching the potential he planned for us and never regretting a moment of it.

② **Sacrifice.** God asks us to sacrifice everything. As we do this, he gives back to us with wisdom and generosity that makes us realize how foolish we were to question our sacrifice.

③ **Servanthood.** As we sacrifice all, we learn how to serve all. This journey of love fulfills us, giving us meaning and purpose and a peace that surpasses our comprehension.

④ **Battle.** We are in the midst of a powerful, life-changing spiritual battle. Each day there are victories and casualties. If we aren't prepared, we become useless. Yet if we are ready, we can wield a force that can have a remarkable impact on today and eternity.

A committed Christian must follow Christ into each of the above areas. Dallas Willard wrote, "The secret . . . is to learn from Christ how to live our total lives, how to invest all our time and energies of mind and body as he did." That's commitment.

Rachel Scott decided to give everything to God. She wrote in her journal that she wanted a true commitment that went beyond just nice words and good intentions. She was hurt when friends rejected her because of this, but she wrote, "I will take it."

On April 20, 1999, another student approached Rachel at Columbine High School. He held a gun to her head and asked her if she believed in God. She looked him in the eye and answered yes. He asked her why, but before she could answer he pulled the trigger. On that day Rachel learned that commitment had a cost. She also proved by laying down her life that she was willing to pay it. Exactly one year before, to the day, Rachel had written the following words in her journal about commitment: "I am not going to hide the light that God has put into me. If I have to sacrifice everything, I will."

Commitment requires a willingness to sacrifice, each and every day. Commitments to marriage and family are noble, but the greatest and best commitment is to God.

TODAY'S TOOLS

Prayer

Dear God,

Teach me to be committed to the things that you are committed to. Forgive me for those times I am only halfheartedly committed or I am committed to the wrong things.

Thank you for the gift of marriage. Help me to be an encouragement in my marriage and in the marriages of those around me. Remind me daily of the importance of affirmation, quality time, nurturing, faithfulness, and honesty. Strengthen me with patience and love so that I can truly love my spouse until "death do us part."

Thank you for my family and the children you have brought into my life—whether I'm a parent, a grandparent, an aunt, or an uncle. Empower me to be aware, assertive, accepting, approachable, affectionate, and alert to all the children in my family. Also prompt me to pray for these children every day, even if only for a moment or two.

Thank you for always being totally committed to me, even when I have ignored or neglected you. Forgive me for the times I've been a convenient Christian rather than a committed Christian. Give me the courage to shoulder my cross and follow you through adventure, sacrifice, servanthood, and battle.

Show me how to be committed.
Amen.

Passage

We urge you in the name of the Lord Jesus to live in a way that pleases God. . . . You live this way already, and we encourage you to do so even more.
1 Thessalonians 4:1

Practice

① If you are married, plan a special date with your spouse. As you prepare for your date, plan three ways you can show your love for your spouse that night. If you aren't married, talk to a couple you admire and share with them one thing you find special about their relationship.

② Think of five ways you can create a memory with a child in your life. Then make plans to do so. When you do, be sure to take plenty of photographs so that you can capture the memory.

③ Make a list of three things you could do to be more committed in some area of your life. Which are you willing to do this week?

RULE ⑮
LOOK FOR LESSONS

GOD TAUGHT ME another lesson today.

A large man with a long scruffy beard and a loud, demanding voice came into my office. His hair was uncombed, his shirt smelled of heavy sweat, and his muddy shoes left tracks across my carpet. I was put off by Tim's arrogant swagger and his order to fix his wife or I'd be sorry. But as we talked, a tear trickled down his cheek when he told me how much he loved his wife and how he was fearful she might leave him. This man who at first appeared hard-hearted was actually quite caring and tender. The longer we talked, the more I liked Tim. But I had to get past my first impression.

After Tim left, I thought of the story of Samuel looking for a king. God said, "The LORD does not look at the things man looks at. Man looks at the outward appearance, but the LORD looks at the heart" (1 Samuel 16:7, NIV). That morning God used Tim to teach me to look beyond the surface and not jump to conclusions. I learned that things are not always as they seem. It's a simple lesson—one I already knew but desperately needed to be reminded of.

Each and every day God teaches me a lesson—frequently many lessons. Some are new and enlightening, and others are reminders of things I had forgotten or had not focused on recently. Some lessons have a heavy impact; others are small and seemingly less significant. Lessons come to us in hundreds of different ways. Yet if we are not keenly attentive, we miss them. In fact, I probably miss much of what God wants to teach me. If God were to send me a hundred lessons in a day and I were to get just one of them, I would consider myself blessed. Looking for lessons requires the intentional determination to get beyond whatever distractions we may face. To find these lessons we must be willing to pay attention, dig deep, and work hard. We don't appreciate what we have found if it is too easy. As Malcolm Muggeridge wrote, "Every happening, great or small, is a parable whereby God speaks to us, and the art of life is to get the message."

On the surface, each day may look random and confusing, but that is frequently because we do not really look and we do not really think. Thinking means connecting things. It involves looking for meaning and wisdom in all we encounter. As a psychologist, I look beyond the obvious to find meaning in my clients' choice of words, facial expressions, style of dress, body language, and a thousand other factors. I look for patterns and purpose in what most might consider random things. Mathematicians find meaning in numbers and algebraic equations. Microbiologists find meaning beneath a microscope. Geologists find meaning in rocks and minerals. There is an order in this universe—an order that provides meaning and millions of amazing lessons. All we have to do is reach out and grab them.

LESSONS IN THE ORDINARY

A poor African farmer worked his land from dawn until dusk each day, barely eking out an existence. In the evenings he heard strange and wonderful stories about great diamonds from travelers passing through—diamonds found beside roads and creek beds. The more he heard of the great riches just waiting for someone to bend down and pick them up, the more excited he became.

One day he sold his farm and went out in search of the diamonds. For years he searched the African landscape, but he found nothing. Eventually he went completely broke, lost all hope, and drowned himself in a shallow river.

Meanwhile, the man who bought his farm faithfully worked his land. After a typical hard day, he picked up an unusual rock and took it home. Several days later a visitor saw the rock on the farmer's mantel and asked him about it.

"There are hundreds of these rocks all over my fields," said the farmer. "This one just has a unique shape."

"Don't you see what you have?" asked the visitor. "This is a diamond."

Sure enough, the original farmer had been standing on acres of diamonds, but he never saw what was right before his eyes. He sold one of the richest diamond mines in the world for just a few hundred dollars. Yet this farmer is like many of us. We miss the lessons right in front of us and go off in search of truth somewhere else.

The ordinary is ordinary only because we have grown used to it. The common, the simple, and the small often hold powerful lessons. Grace Noll Crowell wrote, "The common tasks are beautiful, if we have eyes to see their shining ministry." Laura Ingalls Wilder, author of *Little House on the Prairie*, put it this way: "I am beginning to learn that it is the sweet, simple things of life which are the real ones after all." Yes, it is frequently the things we ignore that can teach us the most. They are the diamonds at our feet.

So don't ignore the little things; don't label anything as insignificant or meaningless. We miss so much that happens around us. In the book of Proverbs, the writer finds wisdom in little animals he observes on an afternoon stroll. He wrote about "ants—they aren't strong, but they store up food all summer" and "lizards—they are easy to catch, but they are found even in kings' palaces" (Proverbs 30:25, 28).

Life's lessons are infinite. In *Letters to Malcolm*, C. S. Lewis wrote, "Any patch of sunlight in a wood will show you something about the sun which you could never get from reading books on astronomy. These pure and spontaneous pleasures are 'patches of Godlight' in the woods of our experience." So look for lessons everywhere. You can find them in the most wonderful and surprising places: in a song or a movie, on the bumper of a car, in a dream, in a smile, on an afternoon stroll, or even in a patch of sunlight.

LESSONS IN ADVERSITY

God sometimes teaches us our best lessons through adversity. In fact, the New Testament author James refers to adversity as an opportunity. He wrote that it has at least seven benefits:

1. It tests our faith.
2. It stretches our endurance.
3. It builds our character.
4. It teaches us wisdom.
5. It prompts us to pray.
6. It reminds us of what really matters.
7. It brings God's blessing.

Trials, troubles, failures, mistakes, and difficulties stretch us in ways that success cannot. Adversity is a powerful teacher. In *A Better Way to Live*, Og Mandino wrote, "Stars may be seen from the bottom of a deep well, when they cannot be discerned from the mountaintop. So will you learn things in adversity that you would never have discovered without trouble." It's interesting to note how many great people have experienced great adversity. George Washington's father died when George was only eleven. Abraham Lincoln's mother died when he was ten. Helen Keller was blind and deaf, and Ludwig van Beethoven became deaf. John Bunyan, author of *The Pilgrim's Progress*, spent years in prison. Walt Disney went bankrupt, and Franklin D. Roosevelt was crippled by polio. Yet through their adversities, each of these people grew braver and stronger. In fact, these very difficulties are part of what shaped them for greatness.

If life is a test, adversities are the hardest questions. Thomas Edison spent years trying to develop a lightbulb, but failure and frustration were his main discoveries. But instead of giving up, he said, "I am now well informed on six thousand ways you cannot do it." Thomas Edison found lessons in his failures, and those failures ultimately led him to success. Pat Williams, senior vice president of the Orlando Magic, wrote, "Your toughest crises are your best opportunities." Adversity is where the greatest lessons take place and the truest growth forces its roots deep into your life.

In the mid-1960s Howard Rutledge, a United States Navy pilot, was shot down over North Vietnam. During his years as a prisoner of war, he was surrounded by death. Through starvation, torture, and solitary confinement he learned many lessons. In his book *In the Presence of Mine*

Enemies, he wrote, "It took prison to show me how empty life is without God." Willa Cather said it this way: "There are some things you learn best in calm, and some in storm."

LESSONS IN PEOPLE

"I met the rudest lady today," said Kristin. "I couldn't believe what she said to me. I'd never say that sort of thing to anyone. It was such a great lesson."

God brings certain people into our lives at certain times with certain words and actions—all to teach us something. Every day I learn amazing things from people. I watch what they do and listen to their stories. I absorb their experiences, their successes, and their failures. Today I learned about patience from Emily, commitment from Al, and the importance of going out of your way from a blind man.

Walking down the sidewalk to a local deli, I saw a man in his thirties with a white cane trying to find his way around a long hedge. I thought about helping, but I was late, and I knew he would sooner or later realize he needed to turn around and go in the opposite direction.

Returning to my office with an afternoon snack, I saw the man again. He was trying to open the door of a shop that had recently gone out of business. "Can I help you?" I asked.

"I think I'm lost," he said. "I'm looking for Mervyn's department store."

I explained that to get to Mervyn's he must go up a half block, turn left and go three blocks, turn left again, and go an additional two blocks, then he'd find it on his right. The man looked confused, so I explained again. He thanked me and hesitantly walked forward.

"Wait a minute," I called. "Why don't I walk you there?"

Suddenly a large smile crossed his face, "Are you sure you wouldn't mind?"

"Not at all," I replied as I gave him my arm.

Later I sat at my desk thinking, *It sure feels good to help others.* Now that's a great lesson that I hope I never forget.

Every person we meet has a story to tell and a lesson to teach. We are surrounded by teachers—wise senior citizens, innocent children, close friends, complete strangers, even enemies and critics. All we have to do is look and listen. Much of what I know is from listening to people's experiences. I learn from what they have learned. I borrow their discoveries and note their mistakes. I memorize what brought them success and do my best to avoid what caused them difficulties. These types of lessons are invaluable.

A thousand lessons stand before you in a thousand different forms. Some are obvious, and some are not. Open your eyes, your ears, your heart. Let your soul always stand ajar—seeking, waiting, welcoming the next lesson. And each evening as you turn out the light and let your head sink into the pillow, review the events of the day. Search for lessons that God has placed along your way—all those messages, both grand and simple, that are easily lost in the rush and clutter but could make your day much more meaningful.

TODAY'S TOOLS

Prayer

Dear God,

Thank you for always being so near and for surrounding me with so many lessons. Thank you that you are a God of meaning and purpose who wishes to share that meaning and purpose with one so small and stubborn as I am.

Forgive me for all that distracts me and keeps me blind to your light and deaf to your voice.

Open my eyes and ears to your marvelous lessons. Help me to see your lessons in the ordinary, the adversity, and the people I meet. Yet most important of all, let me see you and hear you and understand more about you in the midst of every lesson I encounter.

Let me grow richer every day because I have discovered more of the treasure you have meant for me. Make me open to every type of lesson—those that are new and refreshing, those that enforce previous lessons, and those that remind me of lessons I've forgotten.

Keep me awake and alive. Don't allow your lessons to be a point of arrogance or selfishness or independence in me. Rather, teach me to use your lessons to draw closer to you, to walk in your ways, and to glorify your name.

Amen.

Passage

I am the LORD your God, who teaches you what is good for you and leads you along the paths you should follow.
Isaiah 48:17

Practice

① Write out four lessons you have learned through adversity.
② With every person you meet during the next twenty-four hours, ask yourself: What lesson is this person teaching me? How do I feel about this lesson? What can I do to implement what I've learned?
③ Look for God in every lesson. Talk to a friend about what you have learned about God today through the various lessons that have come your way.

RULE ⑯
ACCEPT MYSTERY

JOHN NASH JR. was the most creative and brilliant mathematician in the last half of the twentieth century. At age nineteen he was considered a genius by his professors. At twenty-one he started solving the most complex and perplexing problems in modern mathematics—problems that later earned him the 1994 Nobel Prize in economics. Breakthrough after breakthrough shocked the best minds in the world. At twenty-five he proved the "isometric embeddability of abstract Riemannian manifolds in Euclidean spaces"; nothing seemed beyond the intellectual grasp of this amazing young man. Yet at age twenty-nine, he was struck by paranoid schizophrenia and was soon unable to compose a logical sentence or take care of his own basic needs.

What drove John Nash Jr. to a complete mental breakdown? He believed it was because he was trying to solve one of the greatest mathematical mysteries of all time—what many called the "holy grail of pure mathematics." The intellectual and emotional force required to challenge this mystery ultimately broke him for the next twenty-five years.

Not every problem can be solved, nor every situation understood. The Talmud says, "Accustom your tongue to say, 'I don't know.' " There is much we do not know, and that is okay.

The older I get, the easier it is for me to embrace mystery. Many of the carefully constructed boxes I held to when I was younger no longer hold up to intellectual scrutiny. I don't know as much as I thought I did. I have learned to enjoy the puzzles of life. I have come to relax with obscurity and ambiguity. I live with hundreds of curious paradoxes and thousands of unanswered questions. All these things used to keep me up at night, but now I have given up on figuring it all out. By no means does this mean I have become passive or that my hyperactive curiosity has diminished one iota. It simply means I am at peace with mystery. At times I even cherish it.

Accepting mystery involves embracing that childlike awe and wonder that adulthood seems to steal from us. Maybe this is what Albert Einstein meant when he wrote, "People like you and I . . . do not grow old, no matter how long we live. [We] never cease to stand like curious children before the great mystery into which we were born." Mystery involves excitement and adventure and surprise. What a wonderful way to live. In fact, a life without those qualities is hardly worth living. I have to agree with Harry Emerson Fosdick when he wrote, "I would rather live in a world where my life is surrounded by mystery than live in a world so small that my mind could comprehend it." So let mystery have its place in you.

LIFE AND MYSTERY

Each day of our lives is full of mysteries. I love what Frederick Buechner wrote in *Now and Then*: "Listen to your life. See it for the fathomless mystery that it is." This is a journey of unanswered questions, riddles, wonders, enigmas, and incomprehensibilities. The mysteries of life both woo and terrify. Frederick Buechner also wrote that God provides us all with "momentary glimpses into a mystery of such depth, power, and beauty that if we were to see it head on, in any way other than in glimpses, I suspect we would be annihilated." Too much mystery undoes us; too little mystery denies us. William Blake embraced mystery and in so doing saw life at a deeper level. Therefore, he encouraged all "to see heaven in a wild flower . . . and eternity in an hour."

In order to see the many mysteries that daily surround us, we must learn to value all that creation holds. For when we value something, we are forced to look at it a little closer. And as we look closer at the beauty and intricacies of this life, we can't help but be struck with a certain enchantment. It may seem so simple at first glance, but as we continue to gaze at the world around us, our appreciation is amplified and the mysterious leaves us stunned and surprised. As Fyodor Dostoyevsky taught in his masterpiece *The Brothers Karamazov*, "Love all God's creations, the whole and every grain of sand in it. Love every leaf, every ray of God's light. . . . If you love everything, you will perceive the divine mystery in things." Therefore accepting mystery becomes one of the most joyful and mind stretching of all activities.

This is a marvelous world of magic and mystery. Yet too often we rationalize the magic and fear the mystery. What a terrible shame! It is the mystery of life that makes its adventure so glorious and enticing. The best things in life are the most embedded with mystery, and mystery makes the journey all the more joyful to those who are willing to celebrate the unsolvable and incalculable. One of the most joyful of all writers was G. K. Chesterton. He reveled in mystery, and in *Orthodoxy* he wrote, "We all feel the riddle of the earth without anyone to point it out.

The mystery of life is the plainest part of it. . . . Every stone or flower is a hieroglyphic of which we have lost the key; with every step of our lives we enter into the middle of some story which we are certain to misunderstand." So much mystery, and so much we don't understand. How amazing! As I grow older and wiser, the mystery of life seems to expand rather than shrink.

THE MYSTERY OF GOD

God is a mystery, and the life he gives us is a mystery. Saint Augustine described God as "most hidden, yet most present." Even what we think we understand about God, we don't. Like the apostle Paul said, "Now we see things imperfectly as in a cloudy mirror. . . . All that I know now is partial and incomplete" (1 Corinthians 13:12). No matter how hard we strain our eyes, our view of God is dim and hazy and indistinct. God is infinite in terms of time, space, presence, knowledge, power, perfection, love, goodness, wisdom, justice, and all other things. He is so close we can't focus on him and yet so far away that we can barely see him.

God's ways stretch us beyond our limits. How can we explain the ways of one so mysterious? The best we can do is to make simple guesses as to the mind of the Almighty. "My ways are far beyond anything you could imagine. For just as the heavens are higher than the earth, so my ways are higher than your ways" (Isaiah 55:8-9). As an ant contemplates the Statue of Liberty or the Golden Gate Bridge, so we reflect on God. Saint Teresa of Avila put it simply, "Blessed are those in awe of God." What else can our response be? Yet for the ordinary seeker of God, maybe Jonathan Edwards was right when he preached, "Were

God to disclose but a little of that which is seen by saints and angels in heaven, our frail natures would sink under it."

It all comes down to this: God is so great, and we are so small. Our arrogance and selfishness tempt us to imagine we're bigger than we really are. Our faith tells us to face reality and accept our limitations. Faith involves not fighting with God about the facts. It's accepting that some things don't make sense to us but knowing that they ultimately work out to God's best. To be a person of faith sometimes involves not knowing. As we trust God, we can transform mysteries from points of anxiety or frustration to points of peace and joyfulness. As Dr. James Dobson wrote, "Our task is not to decipher exactly how all of life's pieces fit and what it all means, but to remain faithful and obedient to Him who knows all mysteries."

THE MYSTERY OF MIRACLES

God truly does work in mysterious ways. When I was in college, I drove to Prineville Reservoir to go camping with a few buddies. It was late, and I was driving faster than I should have been. Just before the campsite, the road curved sharply high above the reservoir. When I hit the first curve, I couldn't stay on the road. I slammed on the brakes and spun out in the gravel on the edge of the cliff, but somehow I maneuvered my way back to the road. The next morning I went back to the site to see how close to the edge I'd gotten. In shock I followed the tracks—and saw where all four tires went off the cliff. Ten feet to my left I saw where all four tires returned to the cliff. How in the world had my car gone off the edge without crashing into the reservoir below? There is no logical way this could have happened. It was nothing short of a miracle. It appears that Job was right when he said to God, "I know that you can do anything, and no one can stop you" (Job 42:2).

Miracles are simply those things in life that are unexpected. Dan Wakefield wrote in *Expect a Miracle* that a "miracle is the realm of possibility beyond what we presently know." God isn't limited by our expectations. H. G. Wells wrote that "each moment of life is a miracle and a mystery." In our age of science and rationality, we try to explain away the miracles and mysteries of life. We want control, and miracles force us to acknowledge that we don't have control. We live in a spiritual universe, and we are surrounded by miracles. Every day small miracles take place before our very eyes, but it is only when a larger miracle catches us by surprise that we stand back in awe. Ronald Knox wrote, "Miracles are God's signature, appended to his masterpiece of creation."

We live in a universe where God does the impossible and the unimaginable. When he bewilders us, we call it a miracle. Yet this is simply God showing us his hand. As J. I. Packer wrote, "There is nothing irrational about believing that the God who made the world can still intrude creatively into it." God rules over everything, and his presence is everywhere. Sometimes this presence shines through the commonplace, but we are often too distracted to acknowledge it. Therefore, God sometimes uses the spectacular or miraculous to get our attention. C. S. Lewis described miracles as the "retelling in small letters of the very same story which is written across the whole world in letters too large for some of us to see." The real miracle is that God cares enough to even get our attention.

There is so much we don't understand, but that is what stretches our faith. Pamela Reeve defines faith as "living with the unexplained." I would take it one step further and say that authentic faith embraces mystery. Mystery is like a window through which we may look beyond the walls of this world. Yet what we see when we open our spiritual eyes is unclear, incomplete, paradoxical, and confusing. That is the very nature of mystery. L. Frank Baum, the author of *The Wonderful Wizard of Oz*, wrote, "Never question the truth of what you fail to understand, for the world is filled with wonders." Anton Chekhov, a Russian playwright, wrote, "We shall find peace. We shall hear angels, we shall see the sky sparkling with diamonds." To believe we can or should understand all things is to deprive ourselves of the opportunities available through plunging deeply into the life of faith. When we accept and relax in mystery, we allow peace to sink deeply into every aspect of our lives. As Socrates once said, "You will be gentler and more agreeable to your companions, having the good sense not to fancy you know what you do not know."

TODAY'S TOOLS

Prayer

Dear God,

Let me celebrate the mystery of life, for every day is full of the remarkable. Forgive me for the times when I have ignored, denied, or refused to accept your wonderful, frightening mysteries of life. Thank you for the mystery of birth and growth, the mystery of beauty and power, and the mystery of all that is unexplainable.

You are above all things and the creator of all things. Although you are beyond my comprehension, please help me to grasp some small part of who you are. Let me be amazed by the mystery of you—your infinity, your eternalness, and your majesty.

Open my eyes to the miracles that are all around me. Thank you for intervening in this world with your miracles in times past, and even today. Bring the miraculous into my life to draw me closer to you. Of all the miracles you have ever done, thank you for the greatest miracle of all: that you came to this planet in the form of a man to die a brutal death on a cross, all because of your amazing love. How can I thank you?

Amen.

Passage

Can you solve the mysteries of God? Can you discover everything about the Almighty? Such knowledge is higher than the heavens . . . broader than the earth and wider than the sea.

Job 11:7-9

Practice

① If you could, what three mysteries would you ask God to solve for you? How would knowing these answers change how you live?

② Go to lunch with a friend, and together make a list of as many mysteries of God you can come up with.

③ Have you or someone you know ever experienced a miracle? Ask friends and family members to share examples of miracles in their own lives.

RULE ⓱
SHINE BRIGHTLY

AS GEORGE BAILEY STOOD on the bridge and stared into the icy water, he felt that his life was a failure. It was Christmas Eve, and he believed that the world would be better without him. George had been an example of light in a dark world, but he felt as if it was a wasted effort. At that crucial moment Clarence, an angel trying to earn his wings, shows George what his hometown of Bedford Falls would have been like without his good example and positive influence. His brother would have died if George hadn't been there to save him. His wife would have been a lonely spinster, and the greedy Mr. Potter would have destroyed all that was good in the town.

"One man's life touches so many others," Clarence tells George. "When he's not there, it leaves an awfully big hole."

It's a Wonderful Life has become a holiday classic and one of the most beloved films of all time. Its lesson is timeless: Shine brightly. Be a candle in the darkness. Jesus said, "You are the light of the world—like a city on a hilltop that cannot be hidden. No one lights a lamp and then puts it under a basket. Instead, a lamp is placed on a stand, where it gives light to everyone in the house" (Matthew 5:14-15). George Bailey learned that he made a difference and that in a hundred different ways his light had pushed back the darkness. Edward Everett Hale wrote, "I am only one, but still I am one. I cannot do everything, but still I can do something. . . . I will not refuse to do the something that I can do." Every person has influence, and yours is probably much bigger than you will ever realize. You may only be a small spark of light, but you can make a big difference. Stop for a moment and consider who has shone brightly for you:

- A parent who believed in you

- A teacher who challenged you

- A coach who motivated you

- A friend who stood beside you

You can have the same influence—so use it. William James wrote, "Act as if what you do makes a difference. It does."

As one small candle shines alone in the darkness, it can light another, which lights another—until our corners of the world are ablaze with brightness. Norman B. Rice wrote, "Dare to reach out your hand into the darkness, to pull another hand into the light." It doesn't take a lot to brighten your world—a positive word, a simple smile, a good deed. Let no one encounter you without your parting gift of encouragement and hope. President Woodrow Wilson said, "You are not here merely to make a living. You are here in order to enable the world to live more amply, with greater vision, with a finer spirit of hope and achievement. You are here to enrich the world, and you impoverish yourself if you forget the errand." To shine brightly is to intentionally and boldly stand against the darkness. Boris Yeltsin said it this way: "A man must live like a great brilliant flame and burn as brightly as he can." As we shine brightly, we make a path for others. Through our example we give them a light to find their way. Albert Schweitzer said, "Example is not the main thing in influencing others. It is the only thing." Words of advice might be helpful and powerful, but I have come to believe that people are changed more by the light of example than by anything else.

LIGHTING OUR WORLD

Light is a marvelous thing. Without it we would live sad and limited lives, but with it we are capable of almost anything. When all is dark, we grow cold and confused; we get lost and stumble; we become fearful and anxious. The first chapter of Genesis says, "The earth was formless . . . and darkness covered the deep waters. . . . Then God said, 'Let there be light,' and there was light. And God saw that the light was good" (Genesis 1:2-4). Light wakes us up, ignites us, and energizes us. Light gives us life. It chases away the darkness and opens up a world of possibilities. To bring light into our world is to change everything. Here are eight aspects of light that can make all the difference in our lives and possibly in our world.

Light is truth. Darkness and shadows hide the truth, potentially creating confusion, distortion, misunderstanding, and crisis. But the brighter the light, the clearer the truth. To shine brightly we must hold to the truth, even when it is tough and uncomfortable. Let your light be true and trustworthy. This will draw others to you. As it says in the book of Daniel, "Those who are wise will shine as bright as the sky" (Daniel 12:3).

Light is vision. Without light we cannot see; we are blind to all that is around us. Vision provides clarity, purpose, and direction. Solomon wrote, "Where there is no vision, the people perish" (Proverbs 29:18, KJV). Vision shows us where we are going. Light guides and directs us like a beacon on a rocky shore—guiding us away from danger and directing us toward a safe harbor.

Light is warmth. Bright, sunny days energize me. Cold, cloudy days cause me to bundle up and retreat. Similarly, I am drawn to the light and warmth of a blazing campfire. Light warms me up physically, emotionally, and socially. A smile, a hug, a compliment, a positive attitude, a simple gift, or an encouraging conversation can also provide light that warms me through and through. Lucy Larcom encouraged us all, "If the world seems cold to you, kindle fires to keep warm."

Light is joy. When most people smile, really smile, their eyes sparkle. When people are filled with joy, it seems to shine through their eyes. In fact, the Hebrew word for joy has the root meaning "to shine" or "to be bright." King David wrote, "Weeping may last through the night, but joy comes with the morning" (Psalm 30:5). As the sun breaks above the horizon, chasing away the darkness, there is joy.

Light is courage. As a child I was afraid of the dark. I could imagine some terrifying evil or dangerous monster lurking in the darkness. Yet all my mother had to do was turn on a light, and all was safe. As an adult, I'm aware that the darkness of fear can still grip me. Jim Wallis, editor in chief of *Sojourners* magazine, wrote, "We need the light of courage to face the darkness that lies so thick and heavy before us."

Light is character. Living a good life of love, generosity, and kindness is to be a light in a world of greed and selfishness. Shakespeare wrote in *The Merchant of Venice*: "How far that little candle throws his beams! So shines a good deed in a naughty world." The darker the night, the brighter the light. The apostle Paul encouraged us to "live as children of light" (Ephesians 5:8, NIV). We need to be a candle, a campfire, a lighthouse, anything to chase away the darkness. D. L. Moody said it this way: "A holy life will produce the deepest impression. Lighthouses blow no horns; they only shine."

Light is hope. Without hope, we are lost and forced into despair. Situations might sometimes appear hopeless, but with God there is always hope. In his letter to the church at Ephesus, Paul wrote, "I pray that your hearts will be flooded with light so that you can understand the confident hope he has given to those he called" (Ephesians 1:18). Disappointments and frustrations are limited and temporary. Beyond them, there is always hope—shining brightly and boldly, calling us forward.

Light is faith. Faith is the spotlight that shines through the darkness. It is the greatest light. Chuck Swindoll wrote that with faith "there's no barrier too high, no valley too deep, no dream too extreme, no challenge too great." With faith, all things are possible. Faith allows us to shine. Faith is the light that ignites us, fuels us, and keeps us burning.

SHINE YOUR LIGHT

Each of us is like a candle. Many have never been lit or have been blown out. Others are a mere spark or are flickering, desperately trying to keep burning. Only a few shine brightly enough to light their world and pass that light to others.

It has been said that a thousand candles can be lit from a single flame, but that flame must be bold. Someone once asked Malcolm Muggeridge what he most wanted to do with the rest of his life. His answer was, "I should like my light to shine, even if only very fitfully, like a match struck in a dark, cavernous night."

In a world of darkness, light makes a large difference. People yearn for light, even if they may squint when they see it. I want to be a light shining brightly. But to shine takes more than just well-intentioned words. Don't just talk about light; produce some. Charles Spurgeon wrote that good intentions must be seen: "Lamps do not talk, but shine." Saint Francis of Assisi summarized it all in his famous prayer when he cried out, "Where there is darkness, [let me give] light." And this light will change the world. In one of his speeches, Nelson Mandela reminded us all that "as we let our own light shine, we unconsciously give other people permission to do the same."

Dr. Martin Luther King Jr. was a man who shone brightly. As a leader of the civil rights movement, he was beaten, kicked, and pummeled with eggs and rocks. He was spit at, thrown into jail, humiliated, and threatened, but he refused to retaliate. In January 1956 his house was bombed, and a violent mob gathered, seeking revenge on his behalf. Dr. King spoke to the crowd, saying, "My wife and baby are all right. I want you to put down your weapons and go home. . . . Remember what the Bible tells us: 'Do not be overcome by evil, but overcome evil with good.' "

No matter how unfairly treated or abused, Dr. King was consistent in his words and actions. In a later speech he said, "Do to us what you will, and we will still love you. . . . Throw us in jail, and we will still love you. Bomb our homes and threaten our children, and we will still love you. Send your hooded perpetrators of violence into our communities at the midnight hours, and drag us out on some wayside road and beat us and leave us half dead; and as difficult as it is, we will still love you."

In 1964 Dr. King was awarded the Nobel Peace Prize. He continued to speak his message of love and nonviolent resistance right up to his death. On April 4, 1968, he was shot down in Memphis, Tennessee, as he stepped onto the balcony of the Lorraine Motel. Years earlier, he'd been asked how he would like to be remembered. He replied that when people mentioned his name, he hoped they'd think that he tried "to give his life serving others . . . to love somebody . . . to feed the hungry . . . to clothe those who were naked . . . to visit those who were in prison . . . to love and serve humanity."

Dr. King, among many others, has influenced and encouraged me so that I might be a light that can in some small way influence and encourage others. In so doing, I pray that others may in turn ignite light within their sphere until someday we can push back the darkness and live in the glorious light of God's goodness.

TODAY'S TOOLS

Prayer

Dear God,

Thank you for all those people you have allowed into my life to influence and encourage me. Thank you for all the examples of individuals whose lights have shone brightly. But thank you most of all for the example of your beloved Son, who gave up everything to model the ultimate meaning of love.

Light my candle and breathe your life on it until it shines brightly. Don't let anything blow it out, and don't let my neglect cause it to fade. Help my light to shine boldly for all to see.

Teach me to let my light shine in such a way that I radiate truth to the confused, vision to the lost, warmth to the unloved, joy to the broken-hearted, courage to the frightened, character to the selfish, hope to the discouraged, and faith to those with a distorted picture of you.

Draw me close to you as the source of all light and the sustainer of every element I wish to radiate. Build my light so that it's strong, that I may shine brightly from this day forward. And when I can no longer shine, take me home to the brilliance of your eternal blessings.

Amen.

Passage

If you are filled with light, with no dark corners, then your whole life will be radiant, as though a floodlight were filling you with light.
Luke 11:36

Practice

① List three people you have the most influence upon in life. How do you influence them positively? negatively? What can you do to make sure that you have a more positive influence in their lives?

② Consider a time in your life when you shone the brightest. Ask yourself the following questions:

> *What ignited you?*

> *What kept your flame burning?*

What caused your light to flicker?

What things threatened to put out your light?

What would reignite you or help you to burn more brightly today?

③ Of the aspects of light listed in this chapter, which ones are easy for you and which ones do you struggle with?

RULE ⑱
NURTURE PEACE

LONG AGO A NOBLE KING offered a great treasure to the artist in his kingdom who could paint the picture that best portrayed the meaning of peace. Hundreds of artists accepted the challenge, and within several months, paintings began to arrive at the royal castle. Special judges carefully evaluated each painting, and soon the three best were set aside for the king's judgment.

The first picture showed a perfectly clear lake. Reflected on its surface were the surrounding majestic, snowcapped mountains. The sky was a beautiful blue with a single fluffy white cloud.

The second picture depicted a young mother standing in a gentle meadow sprinkled with white and yellow wildflowers. In the mother's arms was a sleeping baby, carefully wrapped in a pure-white blanket. The mother gazed into the baby's face with tender, loving care.

The third picture showed a stark and treacherous mountain beneath an angry sky of black, evil-looking clouds. Rain fell and lightning flashed. Down the side of the mountain a waterfall cascaded onto a mass of rugged rocks.

After careful consideration, the king chose the artist of the third painting to win the great treasure. Many of the people of the kingdom were surprised by this choice, but upon closer examination they understood the king's wisdom. For behind the churning waterfall was painted a small, scraggly bush growing out of a crack in the rock. In the bush a mother bird had built a nest. And there, surrounded by stormy weather and turbulent water, sat the mother bird on her nest—in perfect peace.

True peace involves a calm heart, even when everything around us is in turmoil. My dictionary defines *peace* as "a state of quiet or tranquility; freedom from disturbance or agitation." Yet we live in a world of noise and agitation. We race about and fill every moment of our day. We worry and feel stressed out and are surrounded by turmoil. A thousand things, real and imagined, seem determined to steal our peace. Yet we all dream of this elusive state of tranquility. Joseph Conrad, the novelist, wrote, "I take it that what all men are really after is some form or . . . formula of peace." We need peace, for it frees us from worry and allows us to concentrate on what's most important. It gives us a better quality of life as well as a longer life.

PEACE WITH OURSELVES

There are many aspects to nurturing our own inner peace, but it must start with simplifying and slowing down. These are flip sides of the same coin. It is difficult to simplify our lives without slowing down, and we will struggle with slowing down until we simplify. To gain inner peace, one must turn inward. Hannah Whitall Smith wrote, "Where the soul is full of peace and joy, outward surrounding and circumstances are of comparatively little account." Peace with ourselves requires letting go. Henry Miller wrote, "If there is to be any peace, it will come through being, not having." Therefore, we must remove the extra stuff that distracts us, consumes us, and wears us out.

Yet most of us are so overwhelmed with the trivial that we have little time left for the important. Therefore we must simplify and declutter our days.

Booker T. Washington said, "There is no power on earth that can neutralize the influence of a high, simple, and useful life." This is the sort of life that brings inner peace. As we simplify, the words of the apostle Paul can become a reality in our lives: "Let the peace that comes from Christ rule in your hearts. For . . . you are called to live in peace" (Colossians 3:15).

Just as there is more to life than stuff and clutter, so there is more to life than speeding through each day. An old fable tells of a rabbi who saw a man running down a road and asked him, "Why do you run?" The man said he was running after his good fortune. "Foolish man," said the rabbi, "your good fortune has been chasing you for many days, but you are running too fast." Slowing down allows us to catch our breath and absorb the moment. It gives us the time to contemplate, gain perspective, and make peace. There is great value in slowing down.

By simplifying and slowing down, we open the door to inner peace. We have the time and ability to nurture the peace we all desire. That inner peace brings with it gentleness and calm and contentment that radiate throughout every aspect of us. That peace also shines forth to anyone who comes in contact with us. Thomas à Kempis wrote, "First keep the peace within yourself, then you can also bring peace to others." Inner peace becomes outer peace. When we have peace with ourselves, we yearn for and facilitate peace with others.

PEACE WITH OTHERS

Self-interest, with all its variations, steals one's peace. It is as we give to others that we discover the greatest joy and peace. Aristotle said, "The greatest virtues are those which are most useful to other persons." Reaching out and serving others teaches us the power of love. Loretta Girzartis wrote, "If someone listens, or stretches out a hand, or whispers a kind word of encouragement, or attempts to understand a lonely person, extraordinary things begin to happen." As we serve others, our hearts soften, our minds open, our bodies relax, our relationships improve, and our spirits draw closer to God. Albert Schweitzer reminded us that "the only ones among you who will be really happy are those who have sought and found how to serve."

To have and give peace, we must intentionally look for daily opportunities to develop a servant's heart. John Wooden said, "You can't live a perfect day without doing something for someone who will never be able to repay you." These opportunities surround us in hundreds of small ways, wherever we may be. In fact, they are frequently so small that we hardly pay attention to them or consider them seriously. Dietrich Bonhoeffer wrote, "Active helpfulness means, initially, simple assistance in trifling, external matters. . . . We must be ready to allow ourselves to be interrupted by God. God will be constantly crossing our paths and canceling our plans by sending us people with claims and petitions." Service might involve talking on the phone when you'd rather not, inviting someone you don't know very well out to lunch, watching a neighbor's children when you have better things to do, or lending something to someone that might be damaged or never returned.

There is something great and Christlike in humble and sacrificial service to others. In *The Purpose-Driven Life*, Rick Warren wrote that real servants "make themselves available to serve." Service is love in action. It is our best gift to each other. It is the gift of peace because love and service often soften the heart of the receiver. Jim Rohn wrote, "Whoever renders service to many puts himself in line for greatness—great wealth, great return, great satisfaction, great reputation, and great joy." And I would most certainly add: great peace.

In their book *Fearfully and Wonderfully Made*, Dr. Paul Brand and Philip Yancey tell the following story: Shortly after World War II, German students volunteered to help rebuild a cathedral in England that had been nearly destroyed by Luftwaffe bombings. As the work progressed, they came upon a large statue of Jesus with his arms outstretched and a plaque at his feet saying, "Come unto Me." Careful patching could repair all damage to the statue except for Christ's hands, which had been completely shattered by bomb fragments. The workers didn't know what to do. Finally they decided to do nothing except change the message. So even today, many years later, there stands in an English cathedral a statue of Jesus—with no hands. At his feet the plaque now reads, "Christ has no hands but ours."

True Christians do the work of Christ. Jesus said, "The Son of Man came not to be served but to serve others" (Matthew 20:28). For as we serve others, we serve God. And his peace fills us. As Mother Teresa frequently said, "The fruit of service is peace."

PEACE WITH GOD

True and lasting peace can come only from God. Ultimately we must all turn to our heavenly Father for peace. Dante summarized this truth in six simple words: "In His will is our peace." We must let go of our wills and egos in complete surrender to God. Peace is the deliberate release of our lives and all they contain to the will of God. Therefore, every moment of every day, surrender yourself to his wisdom and peace. As the highly respected nineteenth-century preacher Andrew Murray wrote, "May not a single moment of my life be spent outside the light, love, and joy of God's presence and not a moment without the total surrender of myself as a vessel for Him to fill full of His Spirit and His love."

Through complete surrender we discover the reality of God and the wonder of his goodness. Our surrender need not be born out of exhaustion or desperation, though it sometimes is. Surrender may also be born out of love or reason. Saint Therese Couderc wrote, "Oh! If people could just understand ahead of time the sweetness and peace that are savored when nothing is held back from the good God."

The Lord is my peace. He calms my spirit, my heart, my mind. Woodrow Kroll affirmed this idea when he wrote, "If our minds are stayed upon God, His peace will rule the affairs entertained by our minds. If, on the other hand, we allow our minds to dwell on the cares of this world, God's peace will be far from our thoughts." Difficulties and troubles will come throughout the day. They will call to us and try to overwhelm us, but they need not control us. As we surrender our hearts and minds to the one in control of all, we will find an unexplainable calm in the midst of turmoil. The apostle Paul, while in jail and experiencing many challenges, wrote that God's peace "exceeds anything we can understand. His peace will guard your hearts and minds as you live in Christ Jesus" (Philippians 4:7).

PEACE BEYOND OUR UNDERSTANDING

Nurturing peace does not come naturally. Yet once we've discovered it, it seems like the only way that is natural or healthy. So live at peace with yourself. Live at peace with others. Live at peace with God. For peace is the best of all possible worlds. Yet we can find it in this world only if we are willing to glimpse into the next.

Work was hectic and responsibilities were heavy. Horatio Spafford had planned a lengthy vacation in Europe with his wife and three daughters, but there was too much to do. So he decided to stay in Chicago for a few weeks, send his family by ship to Europe, and join them as soon as he could. As his family traveled across the Atlantic, the ship ran into a terrible storm. As the crew tried to navigate the ship through the huge waves, it collided with another sailing vessel. Horatio's wife was rescued and taken to England, where she finally got a message to her husband: "Saved alone."

Horatio was shocked and grief stricken. He took the next vessel to England to be at his wife's side. As he passed over the place where his daughters had drowned, the captain of the ship pointed to where the tragedy had happened. Horatio stared endlessly into the waves, silently praying for peace. Finally a smile crossed his lips as he scribbled the following words on a piece of paper:

> *When peace like a river attendeth my way,*
> *When sorrows like sea billows roll;*
> *Whatever my lot, thou hast taught me to say,*
> *"It is well, it is well with my soul."*

TODAY'S TOOLS

Prayer

Dear God,

You are the maker and sustainer of all peace. Thank you for being the central point of peace in the midst of the confusion and conflict and chaos of this troubled world.

When my mind is uneasy and my heart is troubled, give me peace. Calm me, whatever my situation. Let me not be fearful or anxious, but teach me to walk with a spirit of stillness and peace that shines so brightly that no one and nothing can put it out.

When people threaten harm or bring injury, strengthen me. Help me not let others keep me from your all-surpassing tranquility. Show me how to resolve conflicts, let go of anger, and heal my wounds as well as the wounds I have caused others.

When I can find no peace, draw me close to you. Bring me so near that your will becomes my will. Each day, teach me to fully surrender my mind, my heart, my body, my relationships, and my spirit into your strong, gentle hands.

Let your peace always be my peace.

Amen.

Passage

The mind controlled by Spirit is life and peace.

Romans 8:6 (NIV)

Practice

① When in your life have you experienced the greatest sense of peace? How can you get closer to having that same inner peace all the time?

② List three people who are examples to you of being a servant. Consider how they serve and in what ways their service might give them peace. Using their examples, intentionally do something sacrificial for someone this week.

③ Go back and reread the hymn by Horatio Spafford on page 171. What do you need to do to have this sort of peace? What's stopping you?

RULE ⑲
WATCH YOUR WORDS

EVERY DAY I AM BOMBARDED by thousands and thousands of words. There are newscasts, telephone calls, e-mails, music lyrics, conversations, movie and television dialogue, newspapers, books, radio, letters, billboards, and the list continues. Unless you're alone on a deserted island, you can't escape words.

Words are how we share our thoughts and feelings. They are the means by which we express who we are and reach out to others. Communication is the key to relationships, understanding, and growth. Words shape how we think:

- how we perceive the world

- how others see us

- how successful we will be

- how peaceful we are

- how we relate to others

The great philosopher Ludwig Wittgenstein wrote, "The limits of my language are the limits of my mind." Words are incredibly powerful. The apostle James wrote, "If we could control our tongues, we would be perfect and could also control ourselves in every other way. We can make a large horse go wherever we want by means of a small bit in its mouth. And a small rudder makes a huge ship turn wherever the pilot chooses to go, even though the winds are strong. In the same way, the tongue is a small thing that makes grand speeches. But a tiny spark can set a great forest on fire" (James 3:2-5).

Words are strong, but they are also fickle. They can help or hinder all within the same minute. Aldous Huxley wrote, "Thanks to words, we have been able to rise above the brutes; and thanks to words, we have often sunk to the level of the demons." Words are a paradox. We can say such good words and such wicked words. James concluded his previous thoughts with the following: "So blessing and cursing come pouring out of the same mouth. Surely, my brothers and sisters, this is not right!" (James 3:10).

Winston Churchill once said, "By swallowing evil words unsaid, no one has ever harmed his stomach." We can all think of times we wish we'd kept quiet. Yet once our words have come from our mouths, we can't take them back. And if we are not careful, our attempts to repair a situation can make it even worse. As a child I learned a song that said it well: "Be careful little mouth what you say." A sign in front of a church in Dubuque, Iowa, was even more direct: "Lord, please keep one hand on my shoulder and the other over my mouth."

NEGATIVE WORDS

Far away in the Solomon Islands is a village that practices a unique form of logging. If a tree is too large to be cut down with an ax, the villagers yell at it. A group of men creep up on a tree at dawn and scream at it as loud as they can. They do this for thirty days. Robert Fulghum wrote about this in his entertaining book *All I Really Need to Know I Learned in Kindergarten*. He goes on to say that this yelling kills the spirit of the tree. At the end of the thirty days, the tree dies and falls over. Robert Fulghum insists that this is true, and his conclusion is, "Yelling at living things does tend to kill the spirit in them. Sticks and stones may break our bones, but words will break our hearts."

You can slaughter a person with your words. You can do harm that leaves scars for the rest of that person's life. Mother Teresa said, "Violence of the tongue is very real—sharper than any knife." Words can humiliate and injure deeply. One of my clients, Kathy, still remembers, thirty years later, how her third-grade classmates belittled her. Another client, Sam, cringes, forty years later, at how his father told him he would never amount to anything. Henry Wadsworth Longfellow wrote, "A torn jacket is soon mended; but hard words bruise the heart of a child." As a psychologist, I see daily how hard words can also bruise the heart of an adult. Words can close people down and take away their confidence. Words can do more damage than we ever thought possible.

Dangerous words come in all varieties. Some may sound meaningless and harmless, but they aren't. We must consider how they will be heard by others, not just what our intentions are. Dangerous words often take on a life of their own. The types of words I find most dangerous are

- cruel words
- confusing words
- dishonest words
- offensive words

- foolish words

- explosive words

- empty words

- divisive words

- insensitive words

- discouraging words

- abusive words

- arrogant words

When we use these types of dangerous words, we do great evil. Our pride or naïveté has turned our tongues into brutal weapons. Through these dangerous words, trust can be betrayed, friendships broken, families divided, churches split, and communities fragmented. So please beware, for your tongue has an incredible capacity for damage.

POSITIVE WORDS

"May I speak to your manager?" asked Linda.

The twenty-year-old waitress at the local family restaurant looked a bit shaken but replied politely, "Yes, let me get him for you."

The manager appeared at the table a few minutes later and asked, "What can I do for you?" His professional distance told Linda that he was expecting another complaint from an unhappy customer.

"I just wanted to let you know," Linda began, "that our waitress was wonderful. She was friendly and had a great smile. When my kids couldn't make up their minds about what they wanted, she waited patiently and asked them a few questions. After serving us, she double-checked to make sure we were all satisfied."

The manager was relieved, and the waitress was encouraged. As Linda left, the waitress squeezed her hand and said, "Your words made my day; thank you so much. People only talk to my manager when I blow it or if something is wrong."

Unfortunately, most of us are better at complaining than complimenting. If only we fully understood how powerful our words are! They can build bridges or break hearts; they can give hope or steal peace; they can be a glorious present or a deadly poison. Words can change a person's life. So let's do as Dan Nelson suggested: "As soon as you see someone doing something good, tell him about it."

We all love praise. It encourages us and improves our attitude. Sam Deep and Lyle Sussman wrote in their book *What to Say to Get What You Want*, "Praise is perhaps the supreme interpersonal motivator." So I look for things to praise—effort, motive, accomplishment, attitude, words, and character. The apostle Paul said, "Let everything you say be good and helpful, so that your words will be an encouragement to those who hear them" (Ephesians 4:29). When I think back on the people whose words encouraged, motivated, and affirmed me, I smile. These are the people who helped me through difficult times and lifted me to success when I felt hopeless. Solomon wrote, "The words of the wise bring healing" (Proverbs 12:18). Louis Nizer reflects, "Words of comfort, skillfully administered, are the oldest therapy known to man."

We each can bring healing or harm. And often the failure to heal, when an opportunity avails itself, does damage. I challenge us all to pay attention to opportunities to speak healing. We should follow the advice of Emily Dickinson when she wrote, "If I can stop one heart from breaking . . . if I can ease one life the aching, or cool one pain . . . I shall not live in vain."

Kind words are the best currency in good relationships. Cicero wrote, "The rule of friendship means . . . always using friendly and sincere words." Kind words are uplifting. Neil Eskelin wrote in *Leading with Love* that the five most powerful word combinations in the English language are

1. "Thank you."
2. "Would you, please?"
3. "What do you think?"
4. "I am proud of you."
5. "I love you."

These are just a few of the kind words you can share with friends, neighbors, and anyone you meet. Again Solomon had wisdom on the subject: "Kind words are like honey—sweet to the soul and healthy for the body" (Proverbs 16:24). With a little effort, you will never run out of good things to say. I've come to the same conclusion as Goethe, the famous German playwright: "Be generous with kindly words."

There is a tale of a poor boy who was born with a terribly disfigured face. When most people saw him, they whispered and stared; when children encountered him, they cried in horror; and even the strongest of heart were unnerved when they caught a glimpse of him. This boy would have been doomed if it had not been for his beautiful words. If people heard his voice without seeing his face, they were immediately drawn to his gentle, kind, and refreshing language. So he soon learned to cover his face with a mask and use only positive words. As he became a man, his words brought him great success. By his thirtieth birthday he had become the wealthiest, most respected man in the kingdom. He married a lovely wife who gave him three beautiful children.

One day his wife, who had never seen his face, begged him to remove his mask. "But if I let you see my face," said her husband, "you will no longer love me." She insisted that this was not true. She even said that his failure to show his face was a sign that he neither trusted her nor loved her. For a year she persisted in her request. Finally, on a bright spring morning, with much trepidation, he took off his mask.

His wife gasped, and her husband quickly covered his face. "No!" she said. "Let me look again." Slowly he uncovered his face a second time. His wife sighed and placed a mirror before him. "Do you see?" she said. "Your face is the most handsome I have ever seen." As others in the kingdom saw his face they agreed, and many wondered how an ugly boy became such a handsome man.

Yet the man knew the secret. Beautiful words create a beautiful face. Therefore watch your words. They have great power.

TODAY'S TOOLS

Prayer

Dear God,

Thank you for the miracle of words, especially the positive words you and others have spoken into my life. Thank you that you have given us a means of connecting, communicating, and sharing our thoughts and feelings.

Help me to always watch my words, even when I'm hurt or frustrated or angry. Remind me to think before I speak. Keep me from letting unwholesome words come from my mouth. Forgive me for all the cruel, discouraging, and foolish things I have said. When I fail in this area, please don't let my insensitive language hurt those around me.

Guide me in such a way that my words are helpful, encouraging, gentle, right, pure, refreshing, and gracious. Remind me to say thank you often. Fill my everyday language with kind words and compliments.

Open my eyes to the power of my written words so I might write more letters and notes to encourage others. Teach me to show appreciation, offer congratulations, and share comfort to those in my life.

Make my words beautiful to all who hear them, but especially to you. Amen.

Passage

A word fitly spoken is like apples of gold in settings of silver.
Proverbs 25:11 (NKJV)

Practice

① Is there anyone you have spoken negatively to in the past month? If so, go to that person and apologize for what you said.
② During the next twenty-four hours, make it a point to speak only positive words. Fill each conversation with kind words and compliments.
③ Write three letters or notes to people who need encouragement this week.

RULE ⑳
LEAVE A GREAT LEGACY

"I DON'T THINK we're going to get out of this thing," Todd Beamer told the Airfone operator. "I'm going to have to go out on faith."

And that is exactly what the thirty-two-year-old account manager from Cranbury, New Jersey, did. Todd had left his home early in the morning, before his wife and two young boys were awake. He drove to the airport and boarded his flight for a quick business trip to California. Soon the world was shocked by the unfolding events of September 11, 2001. Two hijacked airliners collided into the twin towers of the World Trade Center, another plane crashed into the Pentagon, and a fourth plane was off course and speeding toward Washington DC, with potential targets of the White House or the Capitol. This last plane was United Airlines Flight 93—Todd Beamer's flight.

On board things looked grim. Four hijackers had control of the plane, and the passengers knew they were going to die. But Todd and two others were determined to try to do something about it. They had heard about the three other plane crashes and decided to overpower the hijackers. "It's what we have to do," Todd said to the operator. He asked her to pray with him. Just before 10:00 a.m., she heard him say, "Are you guys ready? Let's roll!"

Sounds of struggle and screaming, then silence.

The plane crashed in an empty field in rural Pennsylvania.

When Lisa Beamer was asked by reporters about her husband's heroism, she replied, "Some people live their whole lives, long lives, without having left anything behind. My sons will be told their whole lives that their father was a hero, that he saved lives. It's a great legacy for a father to leave his children." In another interview, Lisa said, "Todd lived every day trying to make little decisions that were in line with the big goals he had for his life."

Todd came from a family that believed in legacies. He had four loving Christian grandparents and two strong Christian parents who provided positive life examples. Todd's father, David, put it this way: "Passing the baton of faith was a priority in our home. . . . That's a legacy we didn't take lightly." Summing up Todd's actions on that blue-skied Tuesday morning, his father said, "The reason Todd acted with conviction and courage in those extraordinary moments when Flight 93 was falling to the ground was because he had maintained his integrity and values in the ordinary days of his life."

Life is fragile. You might live to be one hundred, or you might die today. Last week a beautiful, sensitive, thirty-four-year-old woman was walking home from work when a car went out of control and hit her. The impact was so powerful that her heart exploded, and she died instantly. No warning. No words. No time for anything. One moment all was well; the next moment she was gone. Randy Stonehill, a songwriter, said, "I'm gonna celebrate this heartbeat 'cause it just might be my last." Moses wrote, "Teach us to realize the brevity of life, so that we may grow in wisdom" (Psalm 90:12). If you were to die today, what would be your legacy?

- What words would be remembered?

- What actions would be remembered?

- What personal qualities would be remembered?

- What achievements would be remembered?

- What social interactions would be remembered?

We all leave behind a legacy of some sort when we die. To make sure that legacy is positive, we must start by envisioning it.

Rick Warren wrote in *The Purpose-Driven Life*, "God wants to use you to make a difference in his world. He wants to work through you. What matters is not the duration of your life, but the donation of it. Not how long you lived, but how you lived." Abraham Lincoln communicated the same thing when he wrote, "In the end, it's not the years in your life that count. It's the life in your years." Fill your life with good. Set goals for yourself—mental, emotional, physical, relational, and spiritual goals. Stretch yourself to do what seems beyond your reach. Then seek God to make it possible. Robert Kennedy said, "Some men see things as they are and say, 'Why?' I dream of things that never were and say, 'Why not?'" I think we should all say "Why not?" a lot more than we do.

You were placed where you are, with the resources and limitations you have, for a reason. Martin Luther King Jr. said, "Set yourself earnestly to discover what you are made to do, and then give yourself passionately to the doing of it." Don't complain about what you don't have, but shape your legacy with what you do have. Formulate a personal mission statement and use it to shape your legacy. I have found there are four key aspects to any mission statement:

① **Make it clear:** easy enough for a twelve-year-old to understand.

② **Make it concise:** no more than two sentences long.

③ **Make it simple:** elementary enough to be recited by memory.

④ **Make it significant:** so important that it will make a true difference in your life and the world around you.

Before you formulate your personal mission statement, ask yourself, *What do I wish to pass on to future generations?* A positive legacy is a priceless gift to leave behind. It will transcend us and touch those we will never know and see. It will impact the future for either good or evil. As John Ruskin wrote, "When we build, let us think that we build forever. Let it not be for present delight nor for present use alone. Let it be such work as our descendants will thank us." Therefore when you envision your own legacy, consider the following suggestions:

- You loved God.

- You made your marriage the best it could be.

- You took good care of your family.

- You were kind and generous.

- You were a true friend.

- You kept your word.

- You encouraged others.

- You had a great attitude.

- You helped those in need.

- You were a good role model.

- You forgave those who wronged you.

- You left this world a better place.

You might not be able to change your past, but you can certainly change the legacy you leave from this day forward. But you must be proactive. In J. R. R. Tolkien's classic *The Fellowship of the Ring*, Gandalf says to Frodo, "All we have to decide is what to do with the time that is given to us." We need to realize that our day-to-day decisions affect not only the quality of our own lives but the legacy we leave for generations to come. If a person envisions a new legacy and is determined to bring it to reality, it can happen.

One of my goals is to leave this world a better place than I found it. Leaving a positive legacy is perhaps the most important thing we will ever do. Yet to effectively consider this, we must look beyond this life with all its successes and failures. Thomas à Kempis wrote, "It is vanity to be concerned with the present only and not to make provisions for things to come." Randy Alcorn calls this living "in light of eternity." After all, Solomon told us that "God has . . . planted eternity in the human heart" (Ecclesiastes 3:11). We look into the night sky or examine the petals of a wildflower or the fingers of a newborn and catch a glimpse of eternity.

The best legacies are lived with a focus on a reality beyond our current grasp. This life is simply a short layover on our way to an eternal home. C. S. Lewis wrote, "Hope . . . [is] a continual looking forward to the eternal world. . . . Aim at Heaven and you will get earth 'thrown in.' Aim at earth and you will get neither." So let us aim at heaven as we live a life that is worthy here on earth.

God is watching and waiting, desiring that we each leave a great legacy. He will evaluate our legacy and "reward each one of us for the good we do" (Ephesians 6:8). When this happens, I pray that a smile will cross God's lips, that he will place his hand on your shoulder and mine, and that he will say what Jesus said in the parable of the three servants: "Well done, my good and faithful servant" (Matthew 25:21).

TODAY'S TOOLS

Prayer

Dear God,

Forgive me for my failures—for all those times I lived for my ego and my agenda and my glory. Forgive me for all I have done, publicly and privately, that may have harmed my legacy. Teach me to make the most of my time, my opportunities, and my talents.

Help me to envision my legacy as you envision it. Show me how to see myself through your eyes. Clarify my potential. Give me a target and the determination to meet it.

Strengthen and stretch me so that I may turn your vision for me into a reality. Guide me each moment of every hour and every day. Give me life with the fullness you meant it to have, so that I might live it for your glory.

Fill me with your remarkable spirit so I may go the distance, finish strong, and end well. Protect me from all that might damage my legacy. Let me leave this world a better place than when I entered it.

Remind me, wherever I might be, to live in the light of eternity.

Amen.

Passage

I fully expect and hope that I will never be ashamed. . . . And I trust that my life will bring honor to Christ.
Philippians 1:20

Practice

① Set aside at least twenty minutes to write out a personal mission statement. Make sure it is clear, concise, simple, and significant. Then ask a good friend to help you improve it.

② List three things that are currently distracting, diluting, blocking, or undermining your efforts to live your legacy.

③ If you were to die today, what would your legacy be? What would people say about you after you were gone?

④ Write the words "Live in the light of eternity" on a note card and put it somewhere you will see it every day.

TRULY LIVE LIFE

LARRY WALTERS HAD ALWAYS WANTED to learn to fly, but through the years he had just never gotten the opportunity.

One day as he sat outside in his lawn chair, Larry got an idea. He went to a local military surplus store and bought a large tank of helium and forty-five heavy-duty weather balloons. Returning home, he attached the balloons to his lawn chair, tied the chair to the bumper of his Jeep, and inflated the balloons with helium.

What an adventure, he thought. *I'll sit back and enjoy a short, relaxing flight. I don't have a plane, but I've got my lawn chair.*

Larry had a BB gun he planned to use to shoot a few balloons when he was ready to return home. Then he sat in his chair and cut the rope connected to his Jeep. *Whoosh!* Larry shot up into the air at a phenomenal speed. His chair flew up and up and up until he finally stopped at some sixteen thousand feet above Los Angeles. Now Larry was a bit nervous. He was fearful of shooting one of the balloons, fearful of shifting his weight, and fearful even of looking down. So Larry just floated above the city—for several hours.

Finally, an airline pilot radioed the Los Angeles airport and informed the air traffic controller that he'd just passed a guy in a lawn chair at sixteen thousand feet with a gun in his lap. A Navy helicopter was sent up to retrieve Larry and bring him back to solid ground. When asked why he'd done something so risky, Larry's response was nonchalant: "A man can't just sit around."

Larry was right in many ways: It's not healthy for people to just sit around. Every day is an adventure, but we must stand up and start the journey. For a day to be great, we must do certain things and follow certain rules. Henry Van Dyke wrote, "Happy and strong and brave shall we be—able to endure all things, and do all things—if we believe that every day, every hour, every moment of our lives is in God's hands." So we can step out with the confidence that God is in control and the determination that we will walk in his ways. As we do these things, we will truly have a great day.

Remember that great days combined make great years, which in time weave into the fabric of a great life. The longer and more consistently you practice these twenty surprisingly simple rules, the richer your day will be. Your life will be renewed, reenergized, and rejuvenated. You will start to live the way God always wanted you to live. As the prophet Isaiah wrote, "You will live in joy and peace. The mountains and hills will burst into song, and the trees of the field will clap their hands! Where once there were thorns, cypress trees will grow. Where nettles grew, myrtles will sprout up" (Isaiah 55:12-13).

So as this small book closes, I hope you take hold of the wisdom collected in its pages. Please don't just read these words only to store them away as something nice and interesting. Let them challenge you and move you to action. Elbert Hubbard wrote, "I believe there is something doing somewhere, for every man ready to do it." What he wrote next is something I hope you can say along with him: "I believe I'm ready, right now."

ALSO AVAILABLE BY DR. STEVE STEPHENS

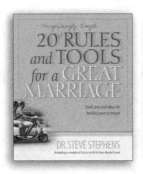 

If you want your family life to be simply great, you'll be amazed at the impact a few simple steps can make. Each book offers twenty clear, to-the-point principles to keep your marriage and your family strong and vibrant. Each chapter includes a prayer to strengthen your relationships and concrete ideas to help you, your spouse, and your kids enjoy each other as never before.

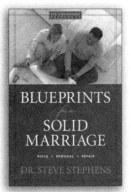

A marriage, like a house, requires time, effort, and regular maintenance. Whether you're in need of light remodeling, minor repairs, or major reconstruction, *Blueprints for a Solid Marriage* offers more than fifty practical projects that will help you quickly assess and enhance your relationship and lay the foundation for marital bliss.